THE HUTTERITES

A
Study
in
Prejudice

DAVID FLINT

Head of the History Department
A. Y. Jackson Secondary School
Borough of North York

Toronto
OXFORD UNIVERSITY PRESS
1975

Maps by GEOFF MATTHEWS
Diagram of a Hutterite colony and
cover design by FRED HUFFMAN

ISBN 0-19-540230-8

Printed in Canada by
THE BRYANT PRESS LIMITED

THE HUTTERITES

A

Study

in

Prejudice

CONTENTS

PHOTOGRAPH CREDITS

PREFACE

The Hutterites are a pacifist communal-living Christian sect that immigrated to North America a hundred years ago. They have drawn much interest from Canadians and Americans. In 1899 a Canadian government official labelled Hutterites as 'the most desirable class of settlers'. Neighbours of their communes have spoken of them as 'a good, hard-working bunch', 'a friendly people' who 'bother nobody'. Sympathetic newspapermen have called them 'the last of the utopian experimenters', 'plainly dressed re-treatants from the world', and 'the most law-abiding people on earth'. But not all of this interest is friendly—the Hutterites have also had many enemies. In 1920 a Manitoba government official said that 'it is the general opinion of this Province that the Hutter-ites should never have been admitted to Canada.' Others have claimed that they are 'an ignorant people', a 'nepotic corporation' who are 'not good citizens'. They have been referred to, scornfully, as 'those people'.

Hutterites speak of themselves as 'the Community of all Be-lievers' and as 'the only true Communists in the world' who could not possibly share with each other in their communal life if they were not dedicated to God and under religious obedience to follow Christ's commands as recorded in the Bible. They believe that they are a fellowship of those who are ready to 'give all' and 'forsake all' in their devotion to the service of Jesus Christ. Hutterites do not want most of the privileges of the modern state—old-age pensions, unemployment insurance, government welfare, or the right to vote and to hold public office. Above all they do not want to be assim-ilated and to become an indistinguishable part of a homogeneous nation. They are not missionary-minded and do not aggressively seek converts. But they believe that they are meant to serve as a

Christian 'beacon on a hill' and they offer a welcome to all who search for 'God's peace'. To do this they have steadfastly sought to preserve their cultural and religious uniqueness through hundreds of years of persecution in many places.

This study has been motivated by the desire to produce a text that would be interdisciplinary, useful in more than one course at different levels of reading skill, and that would give a viewpoint on Hutterites and on the problems of minority groups that would enable students not only to achieve understanding but to debate and analyse issues involved in their dealings with the world. A major failing of recent textbooks has been their authors' scissors-and-paste approach (a snippet of this article, a taste of that author's opinions, etc.), which fails to show how conclusions were reached and, inadvertently perhaps, encourages the mistaken assumption that any viewpoint is good as long as it is stated forcibly enough. In this mass-media age we realize more than ever that points of view differ, though we might not understand that value judgements and decisions still must be made and that thoroughness and diligence are needed to marshal evidence in order to reach conclusions about human problems. This book attempts to give a sociological, anthropological, and historical understanding of a tiny minority group; it also offers a method and model for studying other peoples and for learning and coming to some conclusions about them.

Although I bear full responsibility for the book as it now appears, I would like to express my gratitude to Mike Durrant, Kathleen Fraser, Carl Hogg, Lawrence Krauss, Lew Bobb, Professor Jean Burnet, and my editor William Toye, for their very helpful criticisms and suggestions. I would also like to thank students at George S. Henry Secondary School, who initially stirred my interest in minority-group studies and particularly the Hutterites, and my students at A. Y. Jackson Secondary School. Both groups used a draft version of this text and offered their reactions and comments. To the people of Pincher Creek colony I would like to express my appreciation for their warm hospitality and for their continued interest in this project.

Part One

THE COMMUNAL LIFE

Until recently Hutterite colonies were built away from main highways and out of sight in valleys or land depressions. (See page 150 for the plan of a typical colony.)

The clothes worn by these Lehrerleut girls are made on the colony from yard goods bought in bulk.

1

PINCHER CREEK COLONY

As you drive along the deteriorating pavement of the old highway running south-east from the Trans Canada Highway at Cowley, Alberta, to Pincher Station, the beautiful Rocky Mountains loom in the distance to the south-west. The road dips down suddenly, crosses by bridge the crystal-clear Castle River swift-flowing in a gulch-like, almost barren valley, and proceeds up again and on through vast rolling fields of wheat and barley. A few miles further and you come to a small red-and-white sign on the south side of the road that says 'Pincher Creek Colony' and a Texas gate through which a wide prairie trail leads southward and seems to disappear at the crest of a distant hill. Reaching the top of the hill you can see in the distance a cluster of some twenty-five buildings, both large and small. They seem deserted. There are no human sounds, although the clatter of ducks and geese and the baying of sheep break the stillness of the early but still-hot summer evening. Many of the buildings have the typical drab, insul-brick exterior of second- or third-generation prairie-farm operations, and only their unusual number and diversity indicate that this is a community of over ninety Hutterian Brethren.[1]

As you come closer, past the sheep pasture and the chicken barn—which turns out to be an egg and chicken factory housing over 10,000 hens—several men can be seen working on the foundations of a new, almost fully automatic dairy barn towards the south-east extremity of the building cluster. Turning down one of the dirt lanes leading into what now appears to be a small village with multiple-family dwellings in the centre of a diversified agricultural complex, you see a few women in dark kerchiefs and ankle-length dresses moving about in domestic activity. In front of the entrance to one of these dwellings, under a poplar—the only substantial tree to be seen in this windswept locality—are grouped several men, some bearded and some clean-shaven (the latter clearly younger),[2] and a number of children, their curious faces smeared by the juice of the pink watermelon slices they hold in their sticky hands. They are part of the widespread family of Mrs Barbara Gross, a widow for fifteen years who, by her strong will and with the steady support of the entire colony, has successfully raised thirteen children to responsible adulthood, each now sharing in Hutterite life.

Gross family

The youngest unmarried Gross children—Hilda, Ed, Rubin, Susannah, Judy, and Jerry—are outgoing, glad to see new faces and make new friends. They welcome strangers and take pleasure in showing them about the colony, boasting of its accomplishments and explaining their religion. Every door to every house, building, and cupboard is opened without the slightest inhibition or embarrassment, and even the lids of personal hope chests might be lifted to reveal, to diffident visitors, the few treasures that individual Hutterites are allowed to possess.[3]

The children reflect the sociable, earnest, self-giving personality of Mrs Gross who, in the absence of her dead husband—fondly remembered by his sons and daughters as a man who loved children—watches prudently over her family. Three older daughters have married and joined their husbands' distant communes, but the three married sons have brought their wives to Pincher Creek colony, so that Mrs Gross is now surrounded by a dozen little grandchildren as well as by her unmarried sons and daughters. They are an impressively warm and happy family. When Father and Mother are busy or worn out, there is always Grandma or an aunt or uncle to pick up a fallen youngster, to comfort a tired head, or admonish the mischievous. Mrs Gross, while no longer a young woman, still likes to take a turn in the colony kindergarten, teaching the six boys and seven girls fifteen German hymns to be memorized and sung at Christmas.

The Grosses speak as easily and knowledgeably of their family and religion as of their farming; many daily predicaments or social problems are worked out with reference to Bible passages or sermons.[4] The sons in the family of Barbara Gross are very conscious that their dead father's two brothers are colony ministers. Darius —everyone (including the children) at the colony calls him by his first name—is the minister at Pincher Creek and Paul, a noted Hutterite author, is the minister at the daughter colony near Espanola in the state of Washington. In the absence of a father, Barbara's older children naturally worry about the younger. Michael, the eldest son, thought it wrong that the colony allowed the young boys to spend hours on a tractor every day, because their minds could then fantasize and dream about many worldly temptations, which busy work alongside other men would discourage. Michael is the German teacher for the Pincher Creek colony and his task is a formidable one—to teach all the children to read and write High German, the language of Hutterite sermons and history, and of the Bible.[5] The children must be able to read High German before they can hope to understand the rich and extensive literary tradition of the Hutterian Brethren.

Michael's wife, Dora, who grew up in a colony in Montana and rarely sees her family there, has been relieved of her obligatory colony work, as is the custom when a woman turns forty-five. She will continue to help where and when needed, but she is now free to spend more time looking after her own family of five children (the eldest is twelve) and their spiritual welfare, rather than on the often mundane chores of feeding everyone on the colony. The older generation of women are looked upon as the vital force to teach the young the values of the community in an informal way through day-by-day experiences.

Barbara Gross's second son, Paul (named after his uncle), is responsible for the chickens and is called the 'chicken boss'. He and his wife Esther have four small daughters. Like most such parents everywhere, they hope to have a son—sons are vital to the future of the colony.* The Hutterites have the highest recorded birth rate in the world; but colonies that have low birth rates, especially of males, often have financial difficulties because they lack a labour force and an up-and-coming active generation to

* A son, Markus Paul, was born on September 28, 1973.

push the older bosses to try new inventions and techniques.[6] As Hutterite colonies like to be independent of outside society, their men must not only farm in the fullest sense of the word but some must work almost full-time as electricians, carpenters, plumbers, and mechanics. Without men on the colony who are skilled in these trades, trips to town would be necessary and money would leave the colony to pay outside craftsmen. Because sons stay on the colony after marriage, they provide leadership and continuity of faith and practice and become as well helpmates and companions of ageing parents.

Names   Most of the people on this colony are surnamed Gross—although not all of them are closely related. There is also one Reid and one Hofer family. John Reid was raised on a nearby farm and converted from Roman Catholicism twelve years ago; now he is married and has a young family. Actually there are few Hutterite converts;[7] because of the closely knit nature of the sect, there are only about twenty different surnames among the approximately 20,000 Hutterites in the world. Most of these are German (or Tyrolese) and seven—Walter, Gross, Hofer, Wurz, Mendel, Mueller, Wollman—date back to their first communities in sixteenth-century Czechoslovakia. Some other common names are Waldner, Kleinsasser, Stahl, and Decker. Historically minded Hutterites are interested in genealogy and have records whereby nearly every family can trace its ancestry, generation by generation, back to the 1500s.

In daily living neither the elderly nor those in positions of responsibility are distinguished by the worldly appellations of 'Mr . . .' or 'Sir', for even the young use Christian names to refer to adults other than their mother and father. Surnames are simply not relevant in their community because the Hutterites spend almost their entire lives in or around buildings that are only a few yards apart. They eat together in common dining-rooms, worship together, go to colony schools together from their infancy, work closely as adults in the various specialized aspects of the colony farm operations such as seeding, milking, and feeding livestock, and live in contiguous one-and-a-half-storey houses that usually contain separate apartments for four or five families. While the members of each Hutterite family have a distinct individuality and take pride in the personal and family achievements that differentiate them from their fellow colonists, Hutterites commonly use the pronoun 'we', which always means the whole colony—particularly when they talk about economic and religious matters, the subjects of most of their conversations. The Hutterites have made themselves a closely knit people and they diligently seek to maintain their unanimity.

In the outside world families go to great lengths and expense to have their children, homes, and jobs reflect their individual personality and character. In direct contrast the members of a Hutterite colony seek to keep such individuality in check. It is essential that people who must live in close proximity for most of their working hours, every day, and for most of their lives, develop ways and means to prevent jealousies, competition, and rivalry among themselves. Centuries of experience have shown the Hutterites that the colony way of life must train its membership to think first of the total welfare of the community, its families, and its religion, and to play down individual egos. They do this most notably by maintaining uniformity in their dwellings and dress.

Living quarters vary little in exterior appearance or interior furnishing—one dull-red insul-brick four-unit dwelling looks exactly like its neighbours.[8] Colonies like Pincher Creek, however, are building modern housing units that have wood siding—these new houses are painted white with bright-green trim—and are adding septic systems, inside toilets, and running water, so that some families now have more material advantages. The colony not only agrees on the families who will be given these homes but all the adults work together to build them. When finances and time for construction permit, every family will have modern facilities. Until then, however, wash basins and outhouses are accepted.

The interiors of old and new units are almost motel-like in their sameness and in their emphasis on function rather than decor. The unadorned walls are painted an institutionally bland green and the windows are curtainless; however, there are blinds for night-time privacy. The floors are covered with linoleum and are always spotless. The women take care to maintain the colony standard of immaculate, tidy homes. Saturday is cleaning day when the interiors of all colony buildings are thoroughly scrubbed. Basic household possessions do not offer any opportunities for rivalry or show because each family is equally supplied with plainly styled birch or cedar furniture—beds, dressers, tables, and chairs —that is made, whenever possible, on the colony itself and is of high-quality workmanship. There is no padded or upholstered furniture, though Hutterites possess store-bought mattresses and comfortable homemade down pillows and quilts.

In the smaller apartments or the occasional single dwelling (such as the teacherage) there is simply a large bedroom and a bathroom. There is usually a homemade scatter rug beside the bed, and atop the dresser is a linen runner and a few bottles of hand cream, a prayer study book, and a comb. The only mirror is very small and mounted on a wall. Mrs Gross Sr, with a grown family, has upstairs bedrooms for the boys, downstairs bedrooms for the girls and herself, and a sitting or common room that is entered directly from the back door. Obviously a place for friends and family to gather, it holds a chrome-legged table, many matching straight-backed chairs, a sewing corner, an ironing board and iron, a sink, and a few cupboards for such things as a kettle, store-bought cookies, and tea and coffee for midnight snacks. (All the cups and utensils used in the evening are taken to the central kitchen the next morning, washed and dried with the colony break-fast dishes, and returned to the Gross cupboard.) Beneath the patterned linoleum floor of this room is a cellar reached through an outside hatch, in which are kept such things as wine (supplied and stored by the gallon), made in the colony, and watermelons in season that the colony purchases in bulk from the United States.

Dress   Hutterite dress also unites the community and discourages van-ity and an interest in worldly fashion as it is seen in the consumer society outside the colony.[9] The work trousers, shirts of sturdy dark cotton, and boots of the men differ little from the garb of most farmers, except that suspenders rather than belts are usually worn. Their black or dark-blue dress suits, worn without ties, are not fashionable in any city man's terms, nor are their distinctive broad-brimmed black hats. The women make their own ankle-length dark-coloured dresses with matching aprons in the peasant style of their European origin; they also wear polka-dot kerchiefs, socks, and colony-made shoes. All Hutterite girls must learn to sew and some, like Hilda Gross, who is about twenty-two, become experts: she would be a highly paid professional if she lived elsewhere. The hair of Hutterite women, which is seldom cut, is parted down the centre and again from ear to ear. The hair at the back is rolled into a bun. On either side at the front the hair is brought forward and twisted. These twists are then wound around the bun, which also forms a support for a kerchief. A handsome head of hair, though not much of it is seen publicly, is a point of pride. Hilda Gross is often teased by her brothers and sisters for having thin, hard-to-manage hair. The dress and hair of the children are exactly like those of the adults, though bright clothes are more acceptable on the young. (One concession to personal vanity: Hutterites have bright underclothes!) To the Hutterite, dress takes on a theological significance and is a mark of his or her distinctiveness from the world. Not only is the colony set apart geographically and in its life style from urban secular life, but each individual Hutterite must represent that separateness in his appearance—and hopefully in his behaviour.

When the colony breakfast bell sounds at 7 a.m. the women who are not on kitchen duty simply walk to the communal dining-rooms with their families, eat, and return home to prepare for the day's work.[10] The continuous household drudgery complained of by many housewives is simply non-existent in Hutterite society. The women's chores are organized by the Cook (an inaccurate title because she turns her hand to many tasks), who is often the wife of the minister. She takes care to see that jobs considered tedious do not last too long and she pairs unmarried girls (who have finished school, of course) with married women, not only to have the experienced help the inexperienced, but also to be sure of a worker in the event a mother must leave for a while to feed an infant.[11]

A morning in the cucumber patch of sixty-two hundred-yard-long rows might begin at 8:30 a.m. for the sixteen women and the

Women's work

several young girls and boys who choose to help, but there is no competition to see who can pick the most or the fastest.[12] (From their infancy, boys and girls are taught not to compete but always to do their best.) At 9:30 there is a lengthy break for homemade hot dogs, coffee, and Russian beer—a slightly fermented concoction of bits of toasted bread, molasses, yeast, and water—that, in hot weather, is liked for its sour taste and fizziness. Then it is back to work for another hour and a half. Outsiders who come to the cucumber patch keep the women busy by buying the pickling-size gourds as fast as they are gathered: the women can take pride in raising $100 or so for the colony by a few hours' effort. Then they head home for the colony lunch, which has been prepared by other women for 11:40 a.m. The men plan their jobs to coincide with this time, although during harvesting food is taken to the fields so that precious minutes will not be lost.

All meals are communal. The women and men sit at segregated tables of eight or ten, in descending order of age. (Age and status are synonymous.[13]) Children eat with their teachers at a different time and in another dining-room, partly to make food preparation and clean-up easier for the kitchen crew of that week but also to ensure quietness for the adults during their meal. Eating is prefaced by a short prayer or grace said in German by the minister, who eats alone at a separate table.[14] Without conversation, quickly, and with little apparent concern for table manners, the plentiful food, served on tin pie plates, is unceremoniously gobbled up. In less than twenty minutes the minister, almost without warning, recites another prayer and all stand up, finished or not, and walk out. The clean-up crew then takes over. After a short rest period the afternoon chores begin.

The women's colony chores end around 3 p.m. when school is out and the men come around for afternoon tea and something to eat. When the men return to their jobs in the fields, barns or shops, the women are free to do household chores, catch a few winks, wash their hair, or whatever. While some men work after supper, families normally spend their evenings at home together, except for Wednesdays and Sundays when colony worship is held in the schoolhouse. The lack of television and radio makes Hutterites rely on each other for family entertainment, so that games, walks, sing-songs, quilting bees, and neighbourly visits are commonplace. There are many opportunities for reading the Bible and stories of Hutterite history, especially on long, cold winter nights when outside activity is reduced to a minimum. There are no family pets in the colony; parents' affections are directed entirely towards their children.

The activities of the women are usually limited to the so-called 'traditional roles', but some Hutterite girls would prefer to work with machinery, in the colony furniture shops, or on a combine. However, when assistance is needed in these areas the men call on male help from another colony, not on their women. There doesn't seem to be any regulation or deep-seated hostility against a woman's doing 'a man's work' (for many years at Pincher Creek the women did the milking, a chore now assumed by the men with automatic milking machines), so it seems reasonable to assume that if manpower or economic conditions changed, the traditional activities of women could be transformed.

While official Hutterite teaching proclaims the subordination of women to men, a visit with several families in various colonies would soon dispel the idea that Hutterite women are downtrodden. At Pincher Creek, for example, there are numerous dominant and outspoken women, as in any farming community. The colony is so well organized that women have much more free time, companionship, and family life than most of their counterparts in cities. There is no question of women's importance in the community. By precept and example they guide their children in a Christian life and by hard physical work contribute to the financial well-being of the colony. Though men control the official decision-making positions, women can influence any matters in which they have an interest. 'We give advice,' said one Hutterite woman significantly. At Pincher Creek the number of chickens that were raised each year for broilers was radically decreased because the women felt that plucking and dressing thousands of birds three times a year was an intolerable burden along with their many other chores. The women have the most up-to-date equipment the colony can afford for all the kitchen tasks and cleaning. Their modern ovens can bake forty-five huge loaves of bread (12″ x 18″ x 10″ high) at once; a noodle machine produces for Sunday soup; freezers keep berries and vegetables; a walk-in cooler stores sides of beef; modern commercial washers and driers clean and dry the colony clothing.

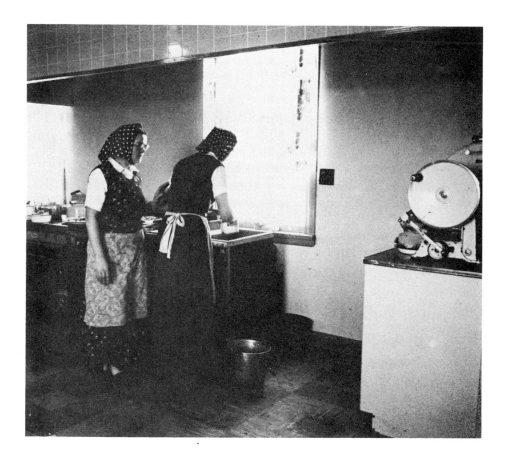

Women's kitchen chores are made easier by many helpers and modern facilities.

(Above) In spite of their dependence on modern technology in other things, the colony women do the washing up by hand.

(Left) The annual killing, plucking and dressing of thousands of poultry a year contributes food and dollars to the colony.

Every generation of Hutterites goes through school and shares all colony activities together. Boys and girls of similar ages eat at one table in a separate room of the communal dining-room and are overseen by the German teacher and his wife. The men and women eat at separate tables and sit according to ascending order of age.

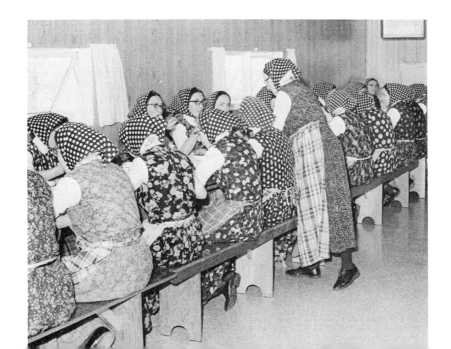

17

Care of the geese and ducks by the women releases men for the mechanical chores of farm life.

18

Some Hutterite families (often newlyweds) have separate houses.

The kitchen and common dining-hall, with a bell on the roof, of a typical Hutterite colony. The building in the centre is a multiple-family dwelling with four entrances.

The
minister

Hutterites look to their religion when making both small decisions, such as how to dress, and large ones, such as the election of their minister, who is the single most important member of the community.[15] Not only does he attend to the spiritual needs of the colony, but his advice is often asked on everything from when the pigs should be marketed to the price that should be charged for eggs. He is the colony leader and his election is the most vital decision the colony makes in affecting its future nature.

To select three candidates for the position, a vote is cast by ballot and those not receiving at least five votes have their names dropped. The final choice is by lot—the man who draws a marked slip out of a hat is considered to be divinely chosen. (Some Hutterites maintain that an elderly minister will groom a relative for the job and that only the ballot box and lottery prevents total nepotism.) The new minister retains most of his previous workload and is also responsible for preaching, the conduct of worship, baptisms, marriages, funerals, and for some teaching as well. He must also recopy old sermons, record family trees, and act as colony spokesman to the outside world. On Pincher Creek colony the minister serves also as garden boss and sheep boss, since these operations are not considered large enough to merit the full-time attention of one man. (Furthermore the minister is a licensed chiropractor and clientele come to him for treatment even from outside the colony.)[16] Ministering to the colony is an onerous lifetime task, yet it is one that some Hutterites covet.

Hutterites expect the minister, even though he has been closely identified with them all their lives, to set standards and demand conformity, and to guard the traditions and values of their religion, and they readily obey him. If the minister is easy-going about slight deviations in dress, the colony will reflect his attitude.[17] On one new colony there was not yet a minister in residence.[18] Dress became sloppy—women went around in summer without kerchiefs and shoes and socks. When asked about this, one embarrassed man replied, 'When the cat's away the mice will play.' He admitted that there was laxity and confessed that this would change when the minister arrived.

Decision-
making

The minister is chairman of the council of elders, made up of the heads or 'bosses' of all the departments of farm production (the machinery boss, the pig boss, the chicken boss). One of the elders, called the Householder, has powers almost as great as the minister's because he has financial responsibility for the entire colony (each colony operates as an independent economic unit) and controls the bookkeeping. Considering that many colonies are worth over a million dollars and that some are in financial difficulty,[19] this can be a perilous position for a man who probably has had no previous banking or accounting experience. The council of elders may decide on general policy and large expenditures for the various areas of production, but individual bosses make day-by-day decisions about their own responsibilities and organize the colony labour to ensure that harvesting and marketing are carried out on time and with efficiency.[20] These bosses, who have been working at their special chores most of their adult lives, carry on trade, make purchases, and sell to the outside community. Paul Gross, the chicken boss, prides himself on his expert knowledge of the chicken-and-egg business and his is a large-scale inter-provincial operation. He is a keen salesman and buyer of one-day-old chickens and boasts the only official government egg-grading licence in all the Alberta Hutterite colonies.

In the week-by-week, year-by-year operation of the colony, group consensus and Sunday-evening meetings play a vital role in maintaining solidarity and discipline. It is an accepted practice to bring pressure to bear on those adults who do not conform to the will of the community. It is considered ethical and necessary to report an individual's misdoings to the colony meeting and this is accepted for the common good and in recognition of the weakness of human nature. Usually the minister will first caution any person who is stretching the colony regulations too far—for instance by showing too much interest in photographs or pictures (considered to be vain), by being overly concerned with one's flower garden (over-watering taxes the limited water supply), or by frequent outbursts of anger. If change is not evident in the person's behaviour, then the preacher and the elders will decide on a punishment. The commonly accepted practice is to have the guilty party stand during church service, or kneel in front of the

Group discipline

entire congregation and confess guilt, or sit with the children.

The ultimate penalty is 'the ban' or 'shunning', but this is rarely used—some Hutterites don't even appear to know the term. It is applied today only to those who leave the colony after baptism. The shunned person is considered dead, and no communication can be carried on with him.[21] This punishment lasts until the sinner publicly repents and re-affirms his baptismal vows; he or she is then accepted back into the colony by the membership. The practical purpose of this ostracism is to bring the wayward, though family-oriented, Hutterite back into the fold; also, those who are thinking of leaving are discouraged from doing so. There is great sympathy among the adults at Pincher Creek for a lost member who has married a non-Hutterite and would like to return but is prevented from doing so because his wife won't submit to colony life.

In cases of minor transgressions against colony rules the minister, as the elected official responsible for maintaining colony discipline, needs deep human understanding to know when and where to draw the line. The question of photographs illustrates the kind of dilemma most colony ministers often experience. 'Hey you! What are you doing? No pictures of the women!' shouted Eli Walter, minister of Spring Creek colony in Montana, to professional photographer William Albert Allard when he found him in the community kitchen photographing the women canning strawberries. 'You know it is forbidden for us to be photographed.' However, though his voice was stern, there was laughter in his eyes.[22] A minister expects outsiders to ask him for permission to take pictures, but he worries that other colonies, or even his own council of elders, will cause a fuss over such laxity. He is also concerned that the young will be tempted by the cameras and other signs of affluence of visitors, or become enraptured by the attention given them by subject-hungry photographers. In their desire to prevent conceit and self-indulgence, some colonies tolerate photographs only if they are put away in the hope chest of personal belongings that every Hutterite is given at the age of fifteen—but even then they are warned against admiring their own likeness. However, colonies that frown on wall decorations often allow pictorial calendars because they have a practical use. It is not unusual, however, to see three calendars in a single room!

The entire Hutterian Brethren Church, through its ministers, constantly tries to maintain religious discipline and prevent the encroachment of worldliness upon community life. Occasionally, however, individual colonies, or Leuts within the sect,[23] disagree with one another over modernization. The first colonies that began using tractors instead of horses, trucks instead of horse-drawn carts, or station wagons instead of trucks, faced possible expulsion from the Hutterian Brethren Church, or certainly much hostility, until the new practice became accepted. At present there is a communal group at Bright, Ontario, called the Brethren of Early Christianity, that contains four expelled Hutterite families from Cardston, Alberta.[24] In New York State, Connecticut, and Pennsylvania, there are three colonies (about 750 persons in total) that were part of the Hutterian Church from 1930 to 1950 before being put out because of their liberal attitudes towards modern dress and smoking and because of their missionary work in industrialized urban areas.[25] These three colonies are collectively called the Bruderhof and many of its adults are from professional or urban family backgrounds and are college educated.[26] In Alberta there are four colonies—Brocket, Monarch, Felgar, and Stirling—that have been cast out by the Brethren even though they still operate in their original location. 'Our forefathers . . . have . . . experienced that when a new generation slips into conformity with the world in non-essential matters, spiritual apostasy follows soon after', states Paul S. Gross.[27] The Hutterian Brethren try to prevent change that they consider will undermine the religious conviction and commitment of their people.

But while the Hutterite religion is slow to change and evolve, the complexity of twentieth-century farming is itself demanding new religious attitudes and ways of life. The Hutterites, who support more people per acre than other Prairie farmers, are always struggling for better land and equipment to be able to increase their profits from livestock production and crops. The Pincher Creek colony, for example, to feed, clothe, and house its ninety-one members, farms 10,000 acres—of which it owns 6,000 acres and

Outside influences

rents 4,000, cash in advance, from the nearby Peigan Indian reserve. The Hutterites would like to be completely self-sufficient and independent of the outside world, yet the very fact that they must farm efficiently such a large acreage makes them dependent upon modern technology, trade, and commerce; they must sell their produce and goods to the local or world markets and buy the latest technology to compete on equal terms with other producers. Their high birth rate makes them dependent on earning large incomes so that money may be saved to start new colonies. Thus they are unavoidably affected by the material values of technological society.[28]

As Hutterites utilize the advantages of scientific farming (they read all the up-to-date farming magazines), and as they drive further and further afield to buy and sell, or to visit other colonies, they become more conscious of the advantages offered by the outside world. There is a growing appreciation of luxury goods and time-saving devices; communities are quick to buy the latest electrical gadgets. Recently the colonies have begun to provide members with a small monthly allowance ($5.00) so that young Hutterites, instead of earning money on the sly from outsiders, can in good conscience make small purchases from town stores.[29] Since community discipline would have suffered by ignoring the money-making transgressors, and since there was a consensus among the membership that small amounts of cash would solve the problem and yet not upset their faith, change was allowed in the traditional way. In line with the communality principle, *all* members were given an allowance. Now that cash is available to Hutterites, even though the amounts are small, society outside the colonies is becoming aware of the Hutterite interest in consumer goods. Salesmen, especially of yard goods, frequent the colonies and, though they can only deal with the boss, are finding a ready market. Even the 'Avon lady' makes an appearance, selling hand lotions, face creams, and clear nail polish (never cosmetics!).

There is growing concern among the Hutterites about the country and its political problems and a genuine interest in outsiders and their skyscraper cities. Some popular magazines are being allowed into the colonies, and educational books and films are now tolerated in the colony school. Hilda Gross writes: 'We read English books. All kinds from the Moody Press Co. We also get the Lethbridge *Herald*, the Pincher Creek *Echo*, which is a paper from our own home town, and all the local news involved. The *Reader's Digest, Free Press Weekly, Country Guide* magazine, the *Western Producer, National Geographic*, and a lot of our nice clean books, but no "trash". We have also shown educational films in our school house for the last 10 years. I know a few titles of some that I can remember. One is about "Land & Soil Corrosion", "How to Prevent Forest Fires", "How to Treat the Wild Life" & "Grizzly Country".'

There is continual pressure for ministers to allow their people to go to town and to visit neighbouring farms (where presumably television can be seen), and they must be wise enough to handle these requests judiciously. The fact that the minister has the keys to the colony's only station-wagon puts him in control of visits outside. Similarly the house of either the Householder or the minister has the colony telephone and, while all can and do use the telephone, indiscriminate calls to town or to neighbours are subtly discouraged. Though Hutterites now allow telephones, visiting, allowances, etc., they have managed to relax their former prohibitions so slowly (and always with common consent) that their religious convictions have not been shaken or undermined by a loss of respect for the authority of the Hutterian Church and its leadership. The actual inroads of the outside world have thus far been petty and relatively insignificant.

Changes in Hutterite attitudes made necessary by participation in the technological world have been paralleled by a new interest in Hutterites and in their way of life on the part of outsiders. With the rise of sociology as an academic discipline, the subsequent popularity of ethnic studies, the acceptability of pacifism engendered by the Viet Nam war, and the growing understanding and tolerance of communal living, the Hutterites have been visited and studied over the last decade by more and more professors, doctoral students, and curious outsiders. At Pincher Creek colony a photographer from Toronto spent two weeks living on the colony, recording on film the life and personalities of the people. One sociologist stayed for days, interviewing and analysing the Hutterites' ethnic identity and religious ethos. A Doukhobor youth from British Columbia came to visit and remained for months as he sought a communal alternative to his own pacifist religion. A Jewish American visited the colony while on a business trip to Calgary and now returns with his wife every summer for a week's holiday. A Lethbridge man whose wife had left him comes every weekend with his two children. Hutterites are pleased that people would travel to their colonies over 2,000 miles from places like Ontario, and are curious to find out what outsiders think and have heard of them. This attention also presents new difficulties and demands new adjustments.

Most Hutterites believe that life on the outside is easy and care-free, an impression conveyed by their contacts outside the colony and by their visitors.[30] They also believe that their communal life —in its stress on daily co-operation, openness, and group disci-pline, and in its downplaying of materialism, individual independ-ence, and ambition—is much more demanding than life outside. It is not surprising, then, that many Hutterite teenagers and young adults, especially those not committed by marriage and responsible jobs to the welfare of the colony, are attracted to the life style of the outside world.[31] The colonies are accepting the fact that young men will take advantage of opportunities to sneak off to town by foot or on horseback—that they will go to movies, smoke behind the barn, and even leave the colony for several months or a year. The Gross boys readily confessed that they enjoyed life outside the colony, but with a touch of pride in their voices they admitted knowing in their hearts that this was wrong and said they would soon give up such behaviour.

'If a boy tells me he wants to leave,' says John Stahl, a liberal-minded minister of another colony, 'I tell him to go ahead, give it a whirl. See if it's better on the outside.' One of John's younger brothers, George, spent almost seven years outside the colony, mostly in the Navy. 'I saw a lot of the world,' he remarked, 'and I met a lot of different kinds of people. But I found that this is the only way for me to live. The big cities, the way people fight and kill each other—that's not for me.'[32] Sam Kleinsasser left his colony at the age of fifteen and wandered around the Canadian and American West working on construction, bronco-busting, and as a migrant farm-worker before returning to become a shoemaker. 'If you live all your life on one of our colonies,' he said, 'you wonder what it's like out there. But when you've been taught from birth until you're fourteen, the whole Hutterite way of living becomes part of you. You can't change that. It's just grown into me, I guess.'

As for the young women, their chores give them little excuse to leave the colony unaccompanied, so that life is much more restricted for them than for their male peers. Paternalistic elders fear that their colony's unsophisticated young women would easily be exploited on the outside, so they are watched more closely than the men.

Without sophistication in the ways of urban living and without a stake to set up a home or business, Hutterites must think carefully before they leave colony life. When a Hutterite wishes to withdraw from a colony, the sect is under no legal obligation to offer any sort of recompense for his contribution. At the Interlake colony in Manitoba, inhabited entirely by nearly related Hofers, four men were expelled by the colony elders (and, therefore, excommunicated from the Hutterian Brethren Church) for refusing to cancel subscriptions to a right-wing fundamentalist magazine originating in the United States. The four men demanded that the courts dissolve the colony and that the $500,000 in assets be divided up. Mr Justice R. B. Dickson ruled 'that the plaintiffs are not entitled to any portion of the real property of the colony; that they . . . permanently vacate the colony and deliver up all personal property owned by the Hutterite colony . . .'[33]

Hutterites always consider their parental or colony responsibilities of childrearing to be finished not when schooling is complete, as do most outsiders, but when baptism and adult commitment to Christ have been undertaken.[34] Baptism is not administered in infancy because they believe that adult baptism is true to the New Testament practice of the free-will commitment to follow Christ and to repent of former evil ways, symbolized by the washing away of sin in the waters of baptism. Young adults of the community are baptized when they finally decide to commit them-

Baptism

selves to the Hutterite faith and to the colony's rules and regulations. This decision is never reached before eighteen and usually after twenty-two years of age.

The formal training for baptism is extensive. A young Hutterite, who has memorized 500 Bible verses and 109 Bible stories by the age of fifteen, studies a sixty-page catechism under the guidance of the German teacher or an assistant minister at Sunday school. Six weeks before the actual baptism, the minister, his assistant, and the colony elders begin intensive two-hour sessions with the neophytes to make sure that they understand the Hutterian view of Christianity and want to join the Brethren. They know that to go back on baptismal vows is unacceptable. (Whereas misconduct is condoned and almost expected from the unbaptized—their escapades of listening to transistor radios and hoarding photographs are conveniently overlooked—post-baptismal transgressions are punished.) On the day before baptism the candidates are questioned intensively about their beliefs. By this time a Hutterite's conscience has been trained by the colony and he is thus enabled to stand firm in the Christian faith. The baptism ceremony is performed on a Sunday afternoon. It is very brief. While the minister places his hand on the person's head and prays that God may preserve him or her in faith and piety until death, an assistant pours a little water on the candidate's head. The young baptized Hutterite has now completed his schooling in obedience—to God *and* to the colony.

Marriage   Often baptism and marriage (the latter cannot precede the former) are closely related in time.[35] Both represent the young person's desire to settle down and to assume full adult responsibilities. To prevent inbreeding, Hutterites do not marry a person from their own colony. Most marriages occur among members of colonies that are close geographically or have family or business relationships. To ensure marital compatibility, Hutterites rarely wed outside their own Leut (a Leut is a group of colonies).[36] To the outsider the differences between Leuts are insignificant, but the Hutterites consider them to be acute. An uninformed stranger would hardly notice that the Dariusleut women have retained the ankle-length dark skirts and blouses of their European ancestry, while the Schmiedeleut women often wear white blouses and white caps that are Mennonite in appearance. The Lehrerleut clothing is more brightly coloured and the women's kerchiefs have larger polka dots. When one Dariusleut girl was asked if she would marry into another Leut, she blushed vividly and said, 'Never! Why, they dress so funny! I'd just as soon not get married.'[37]

From their early teens boys and girls are introduced to their peers in other colonies. Boys and young men help other colonies that need labour, field hands, or extra machine operators. (Eighteen-year-old Jerry—for Jeremiah—Gross spent a month helping to combine potatoes at the colony in Espanola, Washington.) The young women spend part of their summers in other colonies helping relatives with the younger children of large families so that the mothers can have a rest or be released from their normal chores to help with the extra gardening, canning, and preserving work of the season. Both sexes are out-going and gregarious, especially on the colony. The girls are flirtatious and coy—and are expected to be. Courting consists mostly of playing games, of walking and talking together, and of group sing-songs in which hymns or country and western tunes are sung.

Marriage is a community affair.[38] Colony approval, while rarely withheld, must be given, for each new union can seriously affect the spirit and economy of both colonies. A poor colony may not wish to give up a daughter; a wealthy colony might be reluctant to send a daughter to a poor colony where she might have to work too hard. Nevertheless couples who wish to get married—they often have known each other for five years—usually have the full support of family and friends.

The future bride and groom formally announce their engagement at a solemn church ceremony at the bride's colony. There they exchange vows of fidelity to God and to each other. Next there are congratulations and laughter as the young couple tour the community and are greeted and toasted by every family. A few days later, on a Sunday morning, the marriage takes place in the groom's church. The wedding is quiet and serious. The bride wears blue, symbolizing loyalty, and pledges to 'obey' her husband. He in turn promises to be an example of Christian life to his wife.

The minister sagaciously warns that 'marriage has its share of grief and not every day is filled with happiness'. Afterwards there is a marriage feast prepared and paid for by the colony. There is wedding cake, homemade cherry or raisin wine, beer (but no drunkenness), and courting for young couples. On some colonies, guitars and mouth organs are now permitted and the singing of favourite hymns and popular western music tunes adds to the festivities. Hutterites love large gatherings, and family and friends come from far and wide to share in the celebrations and rejoice in seeing each other again. Often two or three couples are married in the same ceremony—in which case there is a gathering of many colonies.

The newlyweds, who are allowed a honeymoon period without colony chores, are given their own separate accommodation. The bride brings with her many household goods and furnishings— certainly a new sewing machine, bedding, and fabrics. When the woman joins her husband's colony she leaves behind her friends and family, the extremely close association of some twenty years. The new wife must adjust not only to her husband, whom Hutterites consider to be the head of the house, but to her mother-in-law, who lives close by, often in the same multiple-family dwelling, and traditionally is considered 'over' all the daughters-in-law. A newly married man not only stays where he is accepted and comfortable but his colony status rises with marriage and he becomes eligible for more responsible jobs and for a say in decision-making.

Old age   Of no small importance in the dedicated work of the men and women is the security for old age provided for each Hutterite— 'the big retirement scheme', as one Hutterite put it.[39] Sociologist and anthropologist John W. Bennett attributes the low rate of Hutterite defection partly to this assurance of lifetime care for all. 'Well, it's a pretty good life, you know,' one young Brethren said to Bennett. 'You go away from it once in a while, but you always come back. Where else can you get a good deal like this for a lifetime?'[40] In practice, when the elderly are eased out of positions of responsibility by ambitious young men, there is bitterness, as there is anywhere else when this situation arises. But at least older people still have the highest status and respect in the community, a secure home, friends, food, clothing, and shelter for life. They know their loved ones will be cared for by the colony and that they have only to prepare themselves for eternity. A Hutterite proverb says: 'When a person comes to his end, great faith is more important than great possessions.'

The Hutterite faith places no emphasis on mourning for the dead.[41] Funeral services are simple and take place shortly after death. The deceased is buried in a plain wooden coffin made in the colony. The burial plot, set off by an ordinary wire fence, contains (usually) unmarked individual graves—the earthly resting place of past generations of Hutterite men and women who believed that their simple communal life helped prepare them for their place with God in heaven.

In their fifty years in Canada, Hutterites have founded more than 150 daughter colonies.[42] When the population of a colony reaches 120 to 150 (there are far more births than deaths each year), Hutterian policy demands that it be split in half. This is often called 'branching' and usually takes place (with the Leut's permission) after fifteen to twenty-five years of growth, preparation, and saving by each colony.[43] The Pincher Creek colony reached its peak of population around 1958, when it split and formed a daughter colony near Espanola, Washington.[44] Now the mother colony is working hard to save at least the $15,000 a year needed to buy land, equipment and buildings for another new colony that they expect will be formed within fifteen years.

Branching

Affluent colonies find that larger numbers are more difficult to discipline and that members begin to fall away from the simple, non-materialistic ways of their religion.[45] Too many conveniences and luxury goods seem to undermine the individual's will to keep the Hutterite faith. When a colony's population becomes too large, there are also serious labour problems. Most important of these is a lack of responsible positions open to ambitious young men. Since a limited number of ministers, bosses, and German teachers are needed in any colony, young men are unable to take over from the middle-aged, who are still very fit and competent and have become almost a management élite—they are reluctant to turn over their work to the new generation. Furthermore, some families control the important jobs and try to ensure that when death or retirement creates openings, these positions will be given to close relations. Hence many adults are assigned menial, dead-end chores. It is plain to see why they become restless, less willing to accept colony authority, and why bickering and low morale are ever-present dangers.

The net per-capita income of colonies whose resources are limited drops closer to subsistence level as numbers grow above 120. With a mushrooming population, younger families would be forced out of the community into urban areas to seek employment —a disastrous possibility, since Hutterites believe that their religion can survive only in rural communes. Whenever lack of capital prohibits a colony from branching, the Leut may make money available by grants or interest-free loans to ensure that the new colony has a good start. The Hutterites are particularly concerned that new colonies initially have enough land—usually 3,000 to 4,000 acres—to produce sufficient income to pay off debts for the large capital expenditures on buildings and equipment that are needed to support sixty to seventy people.[46] In some cases the Leut may find it necessary to bail out an established colony that is bankrupt, not only because bad publicity and a lowering of the Hutterian Church's credit rating would be unacceptable, but also because the sect believes in mutual responsibility. The Leut considers more than financial questions in debating the setting up of new colonies.[47] One colony, because of the shortage of good land in remote locations, wanted to begin a daughter colony three miles outside Youngstown, Alberta, but the Leut refused permission because of the proximity of the urban area and the temptations that would be afforded the young Hutterites.

The individual colony's decisions about when to branch, the location of the new colony, and who shall join it are made by a consensus of all the membership (although only the baptized men may vote on formal decisions). In all colony meetings no action is agreed upon until complete unanimity has been reached: since each individual Hutterite member is considered to have a relationship with, and knowledge of, God, no decision can be made that ignores the solitary dissenting voice. At the Sunday-evening meetings such things as how the colony's machinery, livestock, and money can be divided without regard for personal animosities, family relationships, or cliques are impartially discussed. When the economic decisions have been made, another minister is elected. The day before moving, the names of both the old and new ministers are put on a blackboard and below each a list of colony members is drawn up—based on the family head's preference for a minister—that takes into account a balance of sex, age, family size, and relationships. Both groups pack their few belongings and the two ministers then draw lots. All are prepared to follow what they consider to be the will of God. The 'losing' group must then unpack, perhaps glad to stay in their familiar surroundings. The others apprehensively load their possessions on trucks and move, sometimes many miles to the new site,[48] and begin the very difficult years of labouring to establish a new colony.

Thus leadership has been exercised, commanding the respect of all, and the people have been consulted. They have had a part in a decision-making process that ensures fairness and equity. In this respect the Hutterite colonies have worked out a true democracy.

NOTES

[1] The Hutterites have been incorporated in Canada as 'The Church of the Hutterian Brethren'.

[2] Traditionally beards must be worn by married Hutterite men.

[3] Hutterites do not knock on doors—a habit that can annoy outsiders when they are called on by well-meaning Hutterites.

[4] For a study of the Hutterite family, see S. C. Lee and Audrey Battrud, 'Marriage under a monastic mode of life: a preliminary report on the Hutterite family in South Dakota' in the *Journal of marriage and the family*, vol. 29 (Aug. 1967), 512ff. See also Karl Peter, 'The Hutterite family' in K. Ishwarin, *The Canadian family* (Toronto, 1971), pp. 248-62.

[5] At the time of the Reformation, Martin Luther's translation of the Bible into High German—the dialect of the high region of central and southern Germany—enshrined this form as the official literary German language. High German is the language of the

Hutterite Bible and of its history and worship.

[6] Robert C. Cook, 'The North American Hutterites' in *Population bulletin*, vol. 10 (Dec. 1954), 97-107.

[7] Most converts in Russia and North America have been Mennonites. For further discussion, see Paul S. Gross, *The Hutterite way: the inside story of the life, customs, religion and traditions of the Hutterites* (Saskatoon, 1965), p. 116ff.

[8] The use of space and its importance in the Hutterite community has been examined by John A. Hostetler and Gertrude Enders Huntington in *The Hutterites in North America* (New York, 1967), p. 18ff.

[9] For further discussion, see Gross, *op. cit.*, p. 128ff., and William Albert Allard, 'The Hutterites, plain people of the west' in *National geographic*, vol. 138, no. 1, 124.

[10] The importance of the planned use of time in Hutterite life is explained in Hostetler and Huntington, *op. cit.*, p. 21ff.

[11] For a comparable theory, see B. F. Skinner, *Walden Two* (New York, 1948). See also Kathleen Kinkade, 'Commune, a Walden-Two experiment' in *Psychology today* (Jan. and Feb. 1973).

[12] John W. Bennett, *Hutterian Brethren: the agricultural economy and social organization of a communal people* (Stanford, Calif., 1967), pp. 199-226, describes and analyses Hutterite labour, management, and farming techniques.

[13] Marcus Bach, *Strange sects and curious cults* (New York, 1962), p. 240.

[14] Hutterites consider this to be a deserved privilege. On some colonies the minister and his wife are given their meals in their own house.

[15] For a study of authority and social control, see Lee Emerson Deets, *The Hutterites: a study in social cohesion* (Gettysburg, Pa, 1939), and Hostetler and Huntington, *op. cit.*, p. 27ff.

[16] Hutterites have a long history of medical knowledge and practice. See Robert Friedmann, *Hutterite studies* (Goshen, Ind., 1961), p. 126ff. and 130ff.

[17] The failure of Hutterite leadership is discussed in Hostetler and Huntington, *op. cit.*, 130-5.

[18] This was a rare situation in which premature branching caused a shortage of manpower and one minister had to care for both the mother and daughter colonies by commuting between them.

19 For an unusual case of financial difficulty, see the Toronto *Star*, May 7, 1966.

20 Hutterite enterprise is thoroughly analysed by John W. Bennett in *Hutterian Brethren*, pp. 227-41.

21 Primitive tribal societies use the same method to maintain group unity.

22 Allard, *op. cit.*, 111.

23 See footnote 36 below.

24 Toronto *Globe and Mail*, July 8, 1960.

25 The Church of the Hutterian Brethren has no formal mechanism to 'put out' anyone. It merely ceases any form of communication—as in 'the ban'.

26 Benjamin Zablocki, *The joyful community: an account of the Bruderhof, a communal movement now in its third generation* (Santa Fe, N.M., 1971).

27 Gross, *op. cit.*, p. 38.

28 For further discussion, see the Government of Saskatchewan document (unpublished), *The Hutterite program: a final report* (1958), p. 39ff.

29 Much against the wishes of the adults, teenagers buy transistor radios and keep them hidden under mattresses or in barns, or in the nearest bluff.

30 The Hutterites' view of the world is explained in Bennett, *op. cit.*, pp. 78-105, and Friedmann, *op. cit.*, p. 92ff. For a Hutterite who saw the difficulty of living in the world, see Theron Schlabach (ed.), 'An account by Jakob Waldner: diary of a conscientious objector in World War I' in *Mennonite quarterly review*, vol. 47 (Jan. 1974), 73-111.

31 The permanent defection rate is three per cent and the temporary rate is seven per cent. See *The easterner*, vol. 21, no. 10 (Nov. 25, 1970). For an opposite Hutterite view see Schlabach, *op. cit.*, 89.

32 Allard, *op. cit.*, 120. See also Hostetler and Huntington, *op. cit.*, pp. 105-8.

33 Toronto *Star*, May 4 and Nov. 17, 1966. See also the Government of Saskatchewan document (unpublished), *Treatment of Hutterian Brethren by the provincial and federal governments: a summary* (1963), p. 10.

34 Hostetler and Huntington, *op. cit.*, pp. 80-2.

35 *Ibid.*, pp. 82-7.

36 As the original three North American colonies multiplied, three different Leuts ('people') or groups of colonies were formed. Today their descendants comprise the Schmiedeleut (the

blacksmith people—named after the trade of their first leader), the Dariusleut (after Darius Walther, their founding spirit), and the Lehrerleut (named after the profession of its originator, who was a teacher). See also Gross, *op cit.*, p. 109ff., and *The Hutterite program*, p. 23ff.

[37] Allard, *op. cit.*, 112.

[38] Bennett, *op. cit.*, pp. 106-40; Hostetler and Huntington, *op. cit.*, pp. 10-11.

[39] Hutterites carried on a long legal and eventually (1974) successful battle with the federal government to be exempted from paying Canada Pension Plan contributions on the grounds that they refused to accept old-age pensions or other government monies and that to force them to belong to the plan was religious discrimination.

[40] Bennett, *op. cit.*, p. 129. See also Hostetler and Huntington, *op. cit.*, pp. 87-8.

[41] Hostetler and Huntington, *op. cit.*, pp. 89-90.

[42] One-third are in the United States. Hutterite expansion is discussed in Hostetler and Huntington, *op. cit.*, pp. 44-7.

[43] Leuts vary in their degree of control over individual colonies; for the most part they only advise.

[44] Toronto *Globe and Mail*, Aug. 1, 1950.

[45] Hostetler and Huntington, *op. cit.*, pp. 100-3.

[46] 6,000 acres would be the minimum in the dryer lands of Saskatchewan and Alberta. As the daughter colony grows in population, more land—possibly up to 15,000 acres—must be acquired to make it an efficient economic unit.

[47] Leut meetings are held irregularly and consider common problems rather than making common decisions that are binding on all colonies.

[48] Availability of land nearly always means that the daughter colony will be quite distant. The Pincher Creek colony branched 400 miles. Rapid transportation on the Prairies was difficult until the last few generations and colony branching before the 1950s had to be much closer to the mother colony, thus leading to a concentration of colonies in certain areas and hostility and suspicion by the non-Hutterite inhabitants.

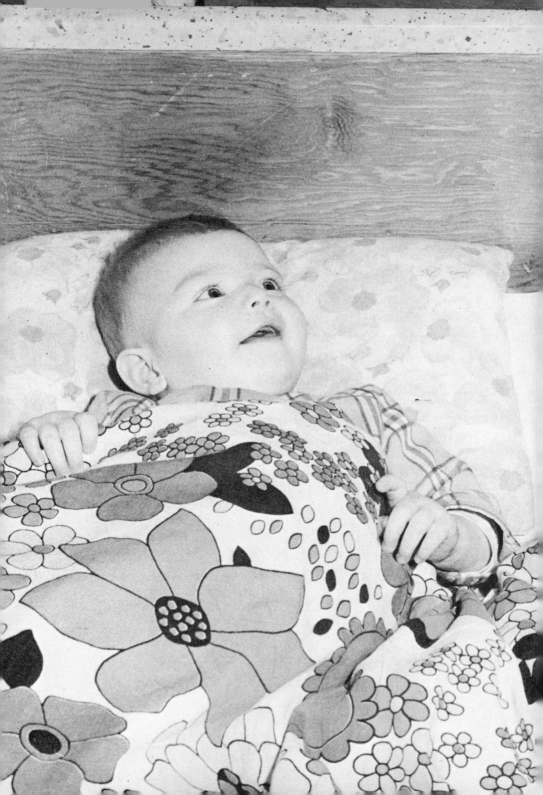

(*Above*) The Klein-Schul room is simple in décor and furnishings, but the atmosphere is affectionate.

(*Left*) While dressing quietly and fairly uniformly themselves, Hutterite parents like to dress their infants and young children in bright clothes and linens.

(Above) A young girl's hair must be braided every morning.

(Left) There is always time for fun at the Klein-Schul and elsewhere during the day.

(*Above*) *A typical Hutterite one-room schoolhouse with desks set in rows.*

(*Right*) *These girls are learning to read.*

Lessons are over for the day at the 'English' school (which is also the church-building) at Pincher Creek colony.

Sewing and embroidery are skills that most Hutterite girls learn at an early age and provide a practical hobby as well for these Schmiedeleut girls.

Youngsters learn much about adult life by being with colony members on and around their jobs. This experience can be fun.

Hutterite boys are fun-loving and adventurous.

2

THE COMMON LIFE

Paul S. Gross writes that the Hutterite way of life 'is not an invention or a social system devised by the Hutterites, nor is it always to their personal liking to live this life. In this they have no choice. They have to live by the command of the Holy Spirit, as we are exhorted by the apostle Peter.'[1] Hutterites are not motivated by a naive faith that rural living will solve twentieth-century problems, nor have they an escapist desire to leave urban life or to flee from pollution. They do not think, as some young intellectuals do, that laws, systems, and institutions have ruined society and that permissive communalism—free love, no rules, no leaders—will create a Utopia. They simply seek to follow the example of Christian living set by the first apostles.[2]

The Book of Acts says that Christ, after his resurrection, instructed his apostles to wait in Jerusalem for the baptism of the Holy Spirit, in which they would be given the power to carry on his ministry to save mankind. On the day of Pentecost—fifty days after Easter—the apostles, and other believers, were all together

when suddenly there came from the sky a noise like that of a strong driving wind, which filled the whole house where they were sitting. And there appeared to them tongues like flames of fire, dispersed among them and resting on each one. And they were all filled with the Holy Spirit and began to talk in other tongues, as the Spirit gave them power of utterance.

This Pentecostal or charismatic[3] experience was interpreted by the apostle Peter as proof that God's spirit was being given to all men through Christ. The purpose and resolve of the apostles was unified and strengthened and they preached fervently to the curious people of Jerusalem (who had heard rumours of the Pentecost's happening). They explained the significance of Christ, his life, death, and resurrection, and demanded of the people that they 'repent and be baptized . . . in the name of Jesus the Messiah for the forgiveness of your sins; and you will receive the gift of the Holy Spirit.' Thousands were converted and they 'met constantly to hear the apostles teach and to share the common life.'

The apostles continued to testify to the power and love of God as proved by the resurrection of Christ from the dead; the number of converts increased and their dedication to God was evident. 'The whole body of believers was united in heart and soul. Not a man of them claimed any of his possessions as his own, but everything was held in common. . . . They never had a needy person among them.' Goods were brought by fellow believers to the apostles, who 'then distributed to any who stood in need'. Converts continued to multiply and their reputation spread. In nearby Antioch they became known as Christians.

The Hutterites, from their first members to the present-day Brethren, have endeavoured to recover and emulate the vitality of the early Christian Church. Their documents show that in 1528, after a group of Protestants was expelled from the Moravian estate of Lord Liechtenstein for not supporting his war effort, they were penniless and destitute. In this time of common need the Holy Spirit moved them to spread their cloaks on the ground and—in the words of the Book of Acts—all 'freely and without compulsion laid his possessions' so that the group's remaining food and belongings would be shared equally. However, a succession of conflicts over group leadership divided them and it was not until 1533—when the forceful and driving Tirolean, Jacob Hutter, convinced them to unite under his leadership—that they emerged as one cohesive, communal religious sect, whose members played down family ties and shared their wealth and goods.

Beginning of communal life

Hutter maintained that true Christianity—the communalism recorded in the Bible—could be practised only in separation from the world, because human nature was materialistic, bound to ac-

quisitiveness, pride, and vanity; only by strong group pressure—
consisting of rules, regulations, and authority—could a Christian
protect himself from these worldly temptations. Hutter was also a
zealous missionary and impelled the group members to go out and
preach their faith to the unconverted. So successful were they in
attracting converts to the sect that the government became
alarmed and persecuted them.[4] At first the authorities tried to
persuade them to renounce their faith or be expelled from their
villages. When this measure had only limited success, capital
punishment was enforced—sometimes by drowning or burning—
at first on the sect's leaders, but eventually against all. It was decided that Hutter should leave his converts for their own safety
and he was hunted for months throughout Moravia, Austria, and
the Tyrol until he was finally captured, tortured on the rack, and
whipped. Still unrecalcitrant, he was burned at the stake as a
heretic in Vienna in 1536.

When the leadership was assumed by Peter Riedemann (1506-
56), few members of the sect earned their living totally by agriculture. Most converts had come from the artisan classes and
many were self-employed as millers, masons, weavers, tool-
makers, supervisors of manors, etc. Riedemann had to guide the
sect through an intense persecution (1547-51) when the Hutterites were forced to live in a maze of underground tunnels in southern Moravia to escape their tormentors. He himself was captured
and spent nine years in prison. While there he wrote, among many
doctrinal and devotional works, forty-five hymns that are still used
by the Hutterites today. He foresaw that commitment to the sharing of wealth and goods could easily disappear when those who
worked hard came to resent giving the fruits of their labour to
those who did little or no work. To avoid this, communities were
eventually set up in which production and consumption were both
shared.[5] They were larger than today's maximum of 150 because
the diverse trades[6] practised brought in more income and there
were more vocational opportunities open to the younger generations.

Twice since the sixteenth century communal living has been
abandoned under external pressure or internal division,[7] but each

time a restirring of Christian conscience has revived it. In North America today it appears to be flourishing. Paul Walter, a vigorous, white-bearded Hutterite minister, describes his Spring Creek colony (Montana) as 'a spiritual ark. Here no one is in need. Everyone helps in the work according to his ability. We believe in glorifying God through hard work and a simple life. . . . Everyone is of equal value to the success of the colony. No man is better than another in our family. We must all work together if we are to survive.' The Hutterites use the word 'Gemeinshaft'—meaning 'the community of spirit of brotherly sharing and togetherness'— to designate the way in which a colony is organized to fashion itself into one large family. In the 1500s they began communal schools to cultivate 'Gemeinshaft' and today they have evolved a communal society that is in itself a school that works to train its members all their lives.[9]

The closely knit structure of Hutterite society is most apparent at childbirth when the community ensures that the mother is entirely relieved of her colony and family work and can spend all her time with the newborn infant.[10] Babies are born in the nearest hospital, and for four weeks after the mother returns home she has only to care for her infant; her own mother and unmarried sisters usually come to look after the housework and others take on her share of the colony chores. The baby is the mother's sole care and she can relax and recuperate from her strenuous pregnancy (during which she would not have been relieved of colony chores) and appreciate the vulnerable new life she has produced. She begins the child's Christian teaching when the baby first takes solid food. She will clasp its tiny hands within hers and say a prayer aloud before feeding time—thus inculcating an attitude of dependence upon God for daily food. Always before bedtime a prayer is recited over the infant, awake or asleep:

Training from birth

> *I am a little child*
> *My heart is pure*
> *In Jesus' name*
> *I go to sleep.*
> *The lovely Angels*
> *Will watch over me.*

Though babies are loved by the entire colony and are always coddled when the adults are not working, they are shown that their wants are not met automatically, for as the mother leaves her dwelling to eat meals or go to church, the baby is left alone in its crib. As she gradually resumes her household chores, the mother leaves the baby alone more and more frequently. One of the characteristics of 'good' Hutterite babies is that they do not disrupt the parents' or the colony's work schedule. The well-regulated common life always comes before a baby's needs no matter how it protests. When the baby is eighteen weeks old the mother resumes her colony work. The infant is cared for by the colony nursery staff and is introduced to its peers and adults outside its immediate family circle. Thus it is gradually weaned away from close dependency on parents to accept its wider Hutterite family.

Education [Rearing children is regarded in Hutterite society as a serious contest between the forces of good and evil, for each child is thought to inherit a sinful nature that can be contained and controlled only by Christian training within the fullness of colony life.][1] 'From the time of a child's birth almost', writes Paul S. Gross, 'the evil element in its nature becomes active. Children will do things which they know they are not supposed to do, and they err in judgement and have within them a covetous will and selfish desires.' Though children are expected to misbehave, question, and rebel, the Hutterites are quite prepared—and expect—to give them years of training and attention so that they will eventually fit into colony life] At the *Klein-Schul*, or pre-school,[12] for ages 2½ (or 3) to 6 years, noisy, often selfish, economically useless youngsters learn to share food with others, to respond positively to Hutterites other than their parents and become adjusted to their own peer group. As the Hutterites have a very high birth rate, there is always at least one child from each family in the pre-school, which is run by an elderly woman and a few part-time younger helpers. The woman is not an academically trained teacher, but her effectiveness is greatly aided by the fact that she knows all the colony families intimately, is often grandmother to many of the children, and has, by tradition, a few well-defined goals in mind. The children eat all their meals in the school (which is usually a small building beside the kitchen), are taught to memorize prayers and simple hymns, for which they are rewarded with candy, and given time to play and to have a midday sleep. They must learn to accept the cramped quarters of the pre-school, the never-changing routine, and the long six-hour day, in preparation for their restricted adult lives on the colony.

The Schmiedeleut allow manufactured toys and play equipment—they believe that if toys are to be allowed, all children should have the same ones—but the other two Leuts regard them as extravagant frivolities. The Dariusleut, however, allow children to bring one small toy from home (at this age youngsters take better care of their personal things), but most of the time they play self-devised imaginative games. (A piece of candy might be fantasized into a combine, a sunflower seed into a truck.) The pre-schoolers are active, run about, poke, wrestle, and tumble with each other. A small playground outside the building might be equipped with swings made from old truck tires. Little supervision is needed, for already the children know that bullying or fighting will not be tolerated. When it is necessary, punishment is administered swiftly and impartially and forgiveness and affection follow immediately. If disputes occur between two children, they soon learn to kiss and hug each other in front of the adults to avoid being disciplined.

Hutterite schooling has actually mellowed from the early sixteenth century when it was first devised. At that time, parents turned their children over to the community and they lived, ate, and slept completely outside the family domain. Andreas Ehrenpreis (1589-1662), who was in charge of the colonies in Slovakia and Transylvania, did much to promote this type of organization by teaching that the true Christian community is one of voluntary surrender and integration of the individual by total submergence in the sect. He used an analogy to wine-making to illustrate his view of Hutterite life.

> . . . *where the wine press crushes each tender berry, each in turn yields all its juice and strength . . . so that the qualities of each single berry are no longer evident, but are part of the whole*

wine. . . . If any single berry escape the press and is not crushed, but retain its own strength and form, it belongs not in the wine, for it is unworthy, useless and is cast out . . .

When the pre-school children turn six, they spend their first year of formal education—four to five hours a day, five days a week—under the tutelage of the German teacher, who meets this group, plus all the children under fifteen, every morning for breakfast at 7 a.m. Children attend the colony public school (English) after they turn seven, but continue to be instructed by the German teacher for an hour before and after school.[13] The responsibility of the German teacher is not only to teach these children to read and write High German in medieval Gothic script but ultimately to give them the background and understanding of Christianity needed for baptism.[14] His curriculum is mostly Bible study and the rote learning of hymns, Bible verses, and stories. This is the content by which the Hutterites hope their children will eventually judge the world, their own community, and themselves.[15]

The German teacher also spends a few hours each Sunday afternoon instructing unbaptized young people over nine years of age. The theme of each Sunday lesson is set by an opening hymn —historical in content—that is then followed by an extemporaneous sermon in which he relates its theme to Bible verses previously memorized by the students. Often these sermons describe the past tribulations of the Hutterites and counsel the children to be prepared to suffer for their faith during their lifetime. He then examines the older students orally on the content of the morning church service, simplifying or explaining parts of the sermon when necessary. The Sunday school closes with the same hymn that was used at the opening.

The German teacher is an elected colony leader who exercises control over his charges outside the classroom as well as in. He teaches them the rules of the colony for the dining-room, and how they should behave in front of non-Hutterite visitors. He shows them how to pray, sing hymns, and sit in church. Moreover, he shows them how to work together in colony jobs. On most colonies the teacher is also a minor farm boss, and if he is responsible for the garden his students help him hoe, plant seeds, weed, or water the plants.[16] Likewise they might be found in the milk shed or the woodworking shop. For the girls a woman is assigned to help the German teacher. While she does not teach German, she shows her charges the adult women roles in the kitchen and dining areas.

Parents also make sure that their children are taught about the community and their place in it. When they are working in and about the colony, fathers are happy to have their young children tag along. They sit in strollers or play with tools and farm gadgets. At nine or ten years children are given small continuing family responsibilities: a girl might look after the family ironing or wash the combine; a boy might be expected to count and sort eggs or pick carrots. In school and during daily work and play, parents watch for signs of natural interest or talent in their children— especially in the boys, for they later specialize in some aspect of farming—so that it can be developed to the colony's advantage. Learning by doing might well be their motto and, except in very rare instances, practical experience is given precedence over booklearning.

The socialization begun in pre-school is continued and intensi-fied as the children grow older. 'The first task,' explains Paul S. Gross, 'is to teach the children to do the things they are supposed to do whether they like it or not, and to avoid those things which they should not do, no matter how pleasant they may seem.'[17] The Hutterites have a pessimistic view of human nature.[18] In demand-ing the unquestioned acceptance of standards, they seek to protect their children—for eighteen years or more—from their natural or inborn selfish instincts. As they grow older this becomes more difficult, especially during the teen-age 'foolish years'.[19] Punish-ment is usually corporal and immediate—a tap on the head, a swat on the behind, or in extreme circumstances a thorough strap-ping—not to hurt him, usually, but to ridicule the child or adoles-cent in front of his peers, or to remind him that he has much to learn about proper behaviour. Never is food withheld or work given as punishment, for both are considered good things and vital to survival. Children are not taught to discipline themselves be-cause they are usually considered incapable of judging right from wrong. Until their character has been trained by their elders over the years, and until they willingly commit themselves as adults to follow Christ and thus overcome their 'sinful' inherited nature, they must accept the authority of those who watch over them and protect them. 'Bend the tree when it is young', runs a favourite Hutterite proverb, 'for you cannot when it is grown.'[20]

Hutterite children are not docile and introverted. They have their pranks and games, their laughter and jokes as do all young people, but they are taught to behave within well-defined boundaries. When the German teacher or the minister, for example, enters a classroom, the children do not cease their noise and chatter, but the moment the willow switch, symbol of authority, is picked up, all quickly settle down. This type of discipline in Hutterite schools is accepted and reflects the attitude of the entire community.

Worship   Worship implements and reinforces day-by-day teaching. In fact the German teacher's aim is to have each of his students actively take part in the colony church services that are attended by all members.[21] There is no special church building and the four weekly services[22] usually take place in the schoolhouse, though any other spacious undecorated room would do. The austere setting is meant to reflect the Hutterite belief in a simple life for all Christians and in Christianity as a religion of the spirit demanding inward change in human nature rather than reaction to, and appreciation of, religious art or ceremony. During the service everyone has his or her place according to the Hutterite concept of authority and deference to age. The elders sit facing the congregation, which is arranged on benches according to age and sex: the youngest in the front seats and the oldest at the back, women on the right and men on the left.

The hymns, prayers, and sermons are all in High German. The sermons are not extemporaneous; on the contrary, most are over two hundred years old and are read or memorized from copies of manuscripts.[23] There is no individualism in the service and all congregational participation is by joint recitation in unison. In contrast to the speed and efficiency of colony meals and work, worship is conducted with great slowness. The minister begins the service by chanting the opening verses of a long hymn line by line—all hymns are verse narratives of the suffering and faith of the Hutterite martyrs—and the congregation unhurriedly returns each line in a clear unison chant. The seventeenth-century sermon is then read in a dull monotone, unembellished by the minister's personal comments or interpretations. In this way the age-old framework of Hutterite belief remains insulated from changing thoughts and cultural patterns. While there are special sermons for times like harvest, most follow a liturgical calendar, beginning with Advent (preparation for the coming of Christ) and ending with Pentecost (celebrating the founding of the Christian Church). The sermon completed, the minister then recites a long memorized prayer that emphasizes the need for God's help to face and overcome the trials and temptations of life. The half-hour service ends with the chanting of the last few verses of the hymn and the minister's benediction. All file out of the building: the older followed by the younger, the men by the women, then the elders, and the minister bringing up the rear as a shepherd to his flock. All proceed to the dining hall 'to break bread together'.[24]

The main outside intrusion into this well-ordered pattern of common religious life has been the public school.[25] Provincial government authorities have insisted that Hutterites pay education taxes and send children under sixteen to a public school, and the Hutterites have complied with these requirements—though as soon as the legal age for leaving school is reached, Hutterite children quit. The local school board appoints a teacher for the colony school, usually from a local community. There have been isolated cases where school trustees have refused to appoint a teacher, claiming that the Hutterite children, like other rural youths, should be sent to the nearest centralized school.[26] In such cases the Hutterites steadfastly refuse to comply, knowing that the long school-bus ride and the lengthened public-school day would destroy their own system of educating their children. Instead they set up a private school on the colony with their own money while continuing to pay normal school taxes. In Manitoba a minimum of ten children is required to obtain a public-school teacher, and so a new Schmiedeleut colony, fifteen miles south-east of Birtle, had

Public schools

to import more families from its mother colony near Lac Du Bonnet two hundred miles away before the beginning of the school year.[27]

A major difficulty encountered by teachers in the one-room ungraded schoolhouse—especially when the outside educational systems are encouraging freedom of expression and the questioning of traditional values—is that the Hutterite elders expect firm discipline to be maintained. Rumours had reached a father that his son was causing trouble for the young woman teacher at the colony school. When he realized that she was doing nothing about it, he marched into class one day, asked if the boy was a troublemaker, and on hearing that he was, immediately put him over his knee and walloped him. Teachers have actually been fired for leniency—a crime Hutterites consider worse than academic incompetence.

Criticism of Hutterite education

Hutterites pioneered pre-schools over 400 years ago, taught hygiene when the practice was relatively unknown, and maintained a standard of literacy unmatched by their social and economic equals until recent times.[28] When their children enter a Canadian public school today they speak two German dialects,[29] are in the process of learning to write High German, and yet quickly become fluent in English at the public school, since all subjects are taught in English. The particular educational system evolved by the Hutterites turns out tri-lingual, law-abiding, family-loving, peaceful, happy, hard-working, productive citizens.[30] Yet in the last few decades educators have unleashed scathing criticism against the Hutterites for their refusal to send their children off the colony to town schools, and against their continued practice of encouraging children to quit school as soon as provincial laws permit, thus denying them mathematical and scientific training and the 'privileges' of modern technological society.

Hostility towards the Brethren was sufficiently widespread in Alberta in 1959 that the provincial government set up a committee to investigate the Hutterites.[31] The committee inquired deeply enough into the Hutterite history and customs to understand them. However, it did not agree with them. The committee felt that the very things the Hutterites tried to avoid in Canadian society—competition, higher education, private ownership, and patriotic attitudes—were the things they needed most. *The Report of the Hutterite Investigation Committee* contains opinions of various school superintendents. One wrote: 'I like Hutterite people but I despise their self-deception. We are dealing with misplaced religious zeal. They won't listen to reason.' Another said that, 'pupils get poorer and more listless as they grow older.' Among the suggestions to break the Hutterites' hold on their children, the report states that 'a . . . subtle approach, aimed at ultimate integration, might be . . . effective. . . . Indoctrination is not recommended but it is felt that Hutterite children would respond well to stimulating teachers with plenty of personality.'[32] In a later section the report complains that Hutterites have 'no loyalty to the country in which they live' (presumably because most colonies do not fly the national flag or sing the national anthem in school—ceremonies considered almost idolatrous) and that 'responsibilities of citizenship are not accepted' (because Hutterites do not vote or hold public office). The report concludes: 'The assimilation of a religious sect exhibiting such strong social cohesion as the Hutterian Brethren will take time and patience.'

Arguments by the Hutterites in support of their educational philosophy have gained little public sympathy and much hostility from professional educators. Those, like the Alberta superintendents, who advocate assimilation of minority groups through the public-school system are naturally most adamant in their opposition to Hutterite educational policy. In this century educational institutions have come to reflect the technological needs of government and business; high-school graduation and university degrees are now necessary prerequisites to join the work force. Even trade unions demand grade-twelve education for apprentices. Individuals—and groups like the Hutterites—who believe in on-the-spot practical education have been ridiculed as reactionaries and semi-literates.[33]

The Hutterites believe that the public-school system should serve their needs as taxpayers and not the supposed educational philosophy of the government. They argue that their young people will spend their adult lives in the agricultural setting of the colony and that the best education for young people after fifteen is in the fields or kitchens, on a tractor, repairing machinery, or learning about cattle. Furthermore, they maintain that night-school and correspondence courses during the slack winter working season can build up any gaps in their academic or technological knowledge as the need arises (although not many seem to take them).[34] Ultimately, however, the Hutterites would assert that education should provide answers to the questions of life through *religion* rather than simply teach one how to do something.

NOTES

[1] Paul S. Gross, *The Hutterite way: the inside story of the life, customs, religion and traditions of the Hutterites* (Saskatoon, 1965), p. 28.

[2] For a description of early Hutterite community life, see Claus-Peter Clasen, *Anabaptism: a social history, 1525-1618* (Ithaca, N.Y., 1973), pp. 260-75.

[3] There is also a twentieth-century religious phenomenon called the Charismatic Movement that seeks to recreate the Pentecost experience. Thousands of people from every Christian denomination, and other religions, have testified that their lives have been changed by an experience of the Holy Spirit.

[4] Clasen, *op. cit.*, pp. 214-43 and 358-442.

[5] John A. Hostetler and Gertrude Enders Huntington, *The Hutterites in North America* (New York, 1967), p. 47ff.

[6] The modern concentration on agriculture arose out of their Russian prairie experience.

[7] For an account of severe persecution during the eighteenth century in Hungary and Transylvania, see John Horsch, *The Hutterian Brethren, 1528-1931, and the principle of non-resistance as held by the Mennonite Church* (Goshen, Ind., 1971), p. 79ff.

[8] William Albert Allard, 'The Hutterites, plain people of the west' in *National geographic*, vol. 138, no. 1, 102 and 108.

[9] For further discussion, see Gross, *op. cit.*, p. 72ff; William D. Knill, 'The Hutterites: cultural transmission in a closed society', a paper presented to the Centennial Conference on the History of the Canadian West (Banff, 1967); John A. Hostetler, 'Socialization and adaptations to public schooling: the Hutterian

Brethren and the Old Order Amish' in the *Sociological quarterly*, vol. 11 (spring 1970), 194ff.; also John W. Bennett, *Hutterian Brethren: the agricultural economy and social organization of a communal people* (Stanford, Calif., 1967), pp. 141-60 and 242-65.

[10] Hostetler and Huntington, *op. cit.*, pp. 58-61, discuss children from birth to two years. For an interesting analysis of the modern communal upbringing of children, see Sonya Rudikoff, 'O pioneers! Reflections on the Whole Earth People' in *Commentary*, vol. 54 (July 1972), 71-2.

[11] See Paul S. Gross, 'Why community?' in the pamphlet *Why community? The Christian community: the idea of communal living*, pp. 4-5.

[12] The Hutterites translate Klein-Schul as 'Kindergarten', but this is not accurate. For further discussion of children from two and a half to six, see Hostetler and Huntington, *op. cit.*

[13] See Gross, *The Hutterite way*, p. 62ff., and Hostetler and Huntington, *op. cit.*, pp. 67-74.

[14] For further discussion of the importance of the German language for the Hutterites, see Hostetler and Huntington, *op. cit.*, pp. 12-14.

[15] Unlike many Biblical 'fundamentalists', the Hutterites do not rely on a few memorized scripture verses on which to hang every idea, relevant or not. They are impressive in their ability to steer nearly every conversation around to Biblical analogies and comparisons in an attempt to relate Christianity to daily-life situations.

[16] At Pincher Creek in summer, when the school is not in session, Michael, the German teacher, can be found feeding the 13,000 geese or laying concrete blocks for the foundation of a new building—or pitching in anywhere else help is needed.

[17] Gross, *op. cit.*, p. 70.

[18] Hillel Schwartz, 'Early Anabaptist ideas about the nature of children' in *Mennonite quarterly review*, vol. 47 (Apr. 1973), 102ff.

[19] Hostetler and Huntington, *op. cit.*, pp. 74-80.

[20] Gross, *op. cit.*, p. 71.

[21] Marcus Bach, *Strange sects and curious cults* (New York, 1962), pp. 248-250; Hostetler and Huntington, *op. cit.*, p. 33ff.

[22] If the minister must be away on business or if the colony is extremely busy harvesting, one or more of these might be cancelled.

Sunday is a convenient day of worship because the outside world keeps it, but to the Hutterites the day of worship is not important.

[23] Friedmann, *Hutterite studies*, p. 184ff.

[24] The women whose turn it is to cook that week are exempt from worship so that the meals can be ready on time.

[25] Hostetler and Huntington, *op. cit.*, pp. 98-100.

[26] See the Government of Saskatchewan (unpublished) document, *Treatment of Hutterian Brethren by the provincial and federal governments: a summary* (1963), pp. 5-8.

[27] The Manitoba government has taken over the responsibility of educating Hutterite children from the local school boards. See *Treatment of Hutterian Brethren*, p. 4.

[28] Friedmann, *op. cit.*, pp. 126ff. and 138ff.

[29] From infancy they speak a sixteenth-century Tirolean dialect, which has been bastardized with Russian and English idioms for everyday use.

[30] Gross, *op. cit.*, p. 47ff.

[31] Saskatchewan also appointed a committee to study the Hutterites. See the Government of Saskatchewan (unpublished) document *The Hutterite program: a final report* (1958), pp. 1-5.

[32] For a similar recommendation with qualifications, see *ibid.*, pp. 50-1.

[33] Critics of education have recently been saying that education should not stop in the classroom. In 1974 the minister of education for Ontario publicly declared that 'More and more we will see students out in the community, in business offices, in museums, in laboratories, in industry, in parks, in downtown areas . . . working and learning.'

[34] Gross, *op. cit.*, p. 59. For some examples of Hutterites in higher education see Allard, *op. cit.*, 117-20, and W. O. Mitchell, 'The people who don't want equality' in *Maclean's*, July 3, 1965. More Hutterites in the U.S. seem to be involved in extension courses than in Canada.

Part Two

A PEOPLE ON THE MOVE

In the sixteenth century various methods of interrogation of Anabaptists included the iron horse, the rack, and stretching with weights.

Rural Alberta residents, mostly from the Vulcan area, gathered on February 28, 1973, on the steps of the Legislative Building in Edmonton, to protest—'quietly', in the words of the Vulcan Advocate—the government's land policy.

3

RELIGIOUS AND NATIONALISTIC CONFLICT

On a bitterly cold day in late February 1973, in Alberta, the most westerly of Canada's vast, windswept Prairie provinces, a cavalcade of 300 angry protesters from the Brant and Vulcan area— 60 miles south-east of Calgary—trekked by car and bus to the government buildings in the capital city of Edmonton, almost 300 miles to the north. Across the province newspapers had proclaimed: 'Stop the land take-over!', 'Save the country from foreigners!', 'Protect our communities!', 'Hostile marchers: violence is feared!'. Letters of hate, abuse, and concern had poured into newspaper and government offices; MLAS[1] had risen in the Legislature and ominously warned that 'people are talking about burnings . . . and taking the law into their own hands.'

This march on Edmonton was undertaken by normally quiet, conservative farmers and small-town businessmen who disliked the pacifist, communal-living Christian sect called Hutterites. They were protesting against the actions of the newly elected Conservative provincial government under Premier Peter Lougheed, who had decided to abolish one of Canada's unique yet controversial provincial laws, the Communal Property Act of 1947, and the subsequent Communal Property Control Board of 1959. These measures had somewhat limited the expansion of Hutterite colonies within the province, threatened their communes with severe internal problems, and encouraged Hutterites to migrate outside the province. Indeed in the last twenty-five years many new colonies had been set up in the province of Saskatchewan and the states of Montana and Washington because of the Alberta restrictions. The Lougheed government believed that the Communal Property Act, passed during the thirty-five-year Social Credit administration, violated the new Alberta Bill of Rights that forbids religious discrimination. The protesters had organized to dissuade the government. In spite of their efforts, however, the repeal took effect on March 1, 1973.

Unlike the Doukhobor zealots—the Sons of Freedom—the Hutterites do not parade nude, make homemade bombs, or set buildings ablaze. Unlike the Seventh Day Adventists, Mormons, and Jehovah's Witnesses, the Hutterites do not address strangers on street-corners or go from house to house ringing door-bells to win converts. Hutterites prohibit card playing, dancing, and smoking, frown on professional sports and games, and discountenance birth control, but they never seek to inflict their notions on others. On the contrary, they avoid confrontations with outsiders and, through their austere standard of personal living and their distinct but plain (usually dark and unadorned) dress, they seek to separate themselves from the world and its fashions. Shrewd agriculturalists and excellent dry-land farmers, they are for the most part unsophisticated. Their success in avoiding many universal social problems is shown by the fact that juvenile delinquency, drug use, suicide, divorce, and unemployment are unknown to them.[2] Wishing only freedom to practise their religion and to act out their belief in communal living, they have nevertheless drawn criticism and hostility from the citizens of all the countries in which they have lived.

No country has tolerated the Hutterites for long nor been able to bring about a thorough cultural assimilation of them. Hutterian Peter Tschetter describes them as 'a people on the move . . . often leaving one land to seek refuge in another. Often they seem to be a people without a country, wanderers on the face of the earth, having no abiding city, and on the whole, pilgrims and sojourners on the earth rather than partakers of the life and culture of the people and nations among whom they have lived.'[3] Behind all the persecution that has attended them for four and a half centuries has been resentment of this characteristic. Most societies cannot tolerate any group in their midst that wants to remain separate and distinct.

The Hutterites are one of the three remaining Anabaptist reli- Early gious groups (the others are the Amish and the Mennonites) that history originated in the sixteenth century during the Christian Reformation in Europe. In common with all Anabaptists of the time, they were persecuted by other Protestants and Roman Catholics for their rejection of infant baptism[4] and for their teachings against the alliance of Church and State.[5] (Both were doctrines that were accepted throughout Europe in the 1500s.) Anabaptists believe the Bible teaches that baptism should be a ceremony of Christian initiation that follows an adult's commitment to Jesus Christ and also that Christians must separate themselves from the sinful world. To remain pure, the Church, as the community of true believers, must not become involved in the corrupting affairs of the State. For example, in the sixteenth century, war and capital and corporal punishment were commonly used by the State even though they were expressly forbidden by Christ's admonitions to be peaceful and non-violent. The Church, when it allies itself with the State, becomes tainted and its divine message perverted. Anabaptists do not want to overthrow the State but want to divorce themselves from its work and methods.

In an era when religious conformity was the accepted norm and when both Roman Catholics and Protestants were violently struggling with each other for supremacy, the challenge of Anabaptism was met head on by the Church, and by the State with which it was in league. In the 1520s and 1530s many hundreds of Anabaptists suffered barbarous martyrdoms.[6] The sentence passed on Michael Sattler, a prominent Anabaptist theologian who in 1528 was convicted of heresy, read in part: '. . . the executioner . . . shall take him to the square and there first cut out his tongue, then forge him fast to a wagon and there with glowing iron tongs twice tear pieces from his body, then on the way to the site of the execution five times more as above and then burn his body to powder as an archheretic.'

Despite these trials the Hutterites, who set themselves apart

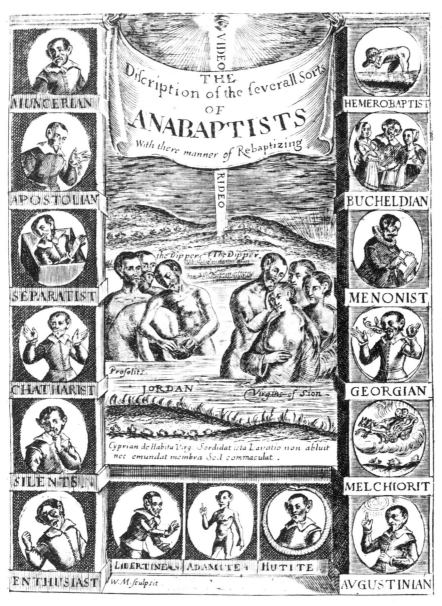

In the seventeenth century the proliferation of Anabaptist sects became a subject for ridicule. This is the title-page of Daniel Featley's Description *of 1645, also known as* The Dippers Dipt.

from the widely dispersed Anabaptist movement in 1528 when they began communal life in Moravia (which was then part of the Hapsburg dynasty's Holy Roman Empire and is now a state in Czechoslovakia),[7] survived. They were able to enjoy such peace and prosperity that they now regard the last half of the sixteenth century as their 'Golden Age'. Membership exceeded 20,000 and Hutterites became renowned as farmers, and for their craftsmanship as clockmakers, shoemakers, cabinet makers, carpenters, potters, spinners, and weavers.[8] Then the Thirty Years' War (1618-48) brought havoc and calamity to all of central Europe. Once again the peaceful Hutterites were victimized, personal atrocities were committed, communes were destroyed and pillaged, and for the next 150 years (until refuge was found in Tsarist Russia under Catherine the Great), the Hutterites declined in number and fortune while wandering eastward through modern Hungary and Romania. In 1770 a tiny faithful band of approximately 100 sought sanctuary near the Desna River in the Ukraine, together with other minority groups that were granted privileges by the Russian authorities in the hope that they would build up the frontier regions of their expanding empire.

For the next hundred years the Hutterites lived freely in the Ukraine; their numbers grew and they prospered economically. However, this very prosperity and the lack of persecution weakened their group resolve to live and work together. In 1819 they gave up their communal life and the common ownership of goods that had characterized their sect from its beginning. If it had not been for the proximity and strength of their fellow Anabaptist neighbours, the Mennonites (who had also sought refuge from persecution in Russia), they might well have been assimilated. The Hutterite saying, 'Good times have never yet made good Christians,' continually reminds them of this unhappy loss of communal life through worldly temptations.

By 1870 many Russian intellectuals and government officials had become caught up in the surge of nationalism that was sweeping Europe. Liberals wanted to make a strong nation. To do so they sought, through public education, to upgrade the masses and to produce a national culture and language with no special privileges for any, but equality (and, therefore, conformity) for all. Minority groups such as the Mennonites and Hutterites were targets of nationalist attacks because they refused to become part of the Russian nation, retained their German language, and, of course, were not members of the state Orthodox religion. There had not been one intermarriage between a Hutterite and a Russian. Completely galling were the privileges that had been given the Hutterites and other minorities in 1770 to entice immigrants; a hundred years later the Russian government abolished their rights to exemption from military service as guaranteed by Catherine the Great and asked that, instead of actual combat, they undertake alternative national service.[9] Also, Russian was to become the compulsory language of instruction in such schools as then existed in Russia—a direct slap at the Anabaptists, who were far more advanced in education than most of their Russian neighbours. Immediately many Mennonites and all the Hutterites decided to leave the country rather than submit to a language policy that might speed up their assimilation and to a military policy that was in conflict with their conscience.

Arrival in U.S. Delegates were sent to investigate the lands and policies of North American governments and in 1873 they visited parts of the United States and the fledgling province of Manitoba in Canada,[10] then inhabited mostly by Indians and Métis.[11] Only Canada would guarantee them military exemption, but one half of the Mennonites (18,000) and all Hutterites (500 to 800) opted for the better lands and climatic conditions of the United States— and hoped that war would never come. A revival of communal ideals had recently begun to form and in 1878, when the Hutterites settled in the James River valleys of the Dakota territory[12]—soon to be the south-east corner of the state of South Dakota—half of them started three colonies. The remaining Hutterites homesteaded as individual landholders and have since been largely assimilated into American society, although many of their descendants belong to the Crimean (Krimmer) Mennonite Church. By 1917, when war fever hit the United States, the communal Hutterites were becoming prosperous; there were seventeen colonies and their numbers had grown to 1,700.

Before the United States entered the First World War, allied propaganda and Americans who were favourable to their country's participation[13] spread the idea in the U.S. that the Germans were militaristic imperialists who committed brutal atrocities, and that Germany was a threat to civilization and democracy. Not all were easily convinced. The recent large European immigration—about 32 million (many of whom had fled Europe to escape warfare)— and a great many people of pro-German sympathies in the Middle West demanded neutrality and pacifism. However, the sinking of American merchant ships in the war zone by German U-boats finally persuaded the United States to declare war on April 6, 1917. Now there was little public sympathy for those who did not join up, much less for those who gave the war no moral or vocal support. The citizenship responsibilities of those who were opposed to war were dramatically brought into question.

In the Selective Service Act of May 18, 1917, conscription was made absolute and universal and the president was granted the privilege of defining noncombatant service. President Wilson announced on March 20, 1918 that pacifists—including the Hutterites—were expected to join the military in a noncombatant role.

The Hutterites had been distinguished for their non-violence since 1528, when they split away from many of their Anabaptist brethren who had accepted wartime protection from a Moravian, Lord Liechtenstein. They believed that an unknown fate at the hands of the invading Moslem Turks would be better than co-operation in a war effort that must disobey the Biblical commandment 'Thou shalt not kill'. Their non-violence resulted from more than the liberal conviction that one culture or nation did not have the right to trample upon a weaker one and went beyond the pacifist conviction that it is wrong to kill people for humanistic or divine reasons. They had a complete disdain of all human physical violence.[14] In the words of Jacob Hutter, from whom the sect takes its name,

Here we lie upon the barren earth, as God wills, without harm to anyone. We do not wish nor desire to do harm or evil to any man, yea, not even to our worst enemy. And all our life and deeds, words and works are open to all. Yea, before we would knowingly wrong a man to the value of a penny, we would rather lose a hundred pounds; and before we would strike our greatest enemy with the hand, to say nothing of with the gun or sword, as the world does, we would rather die, and let our own lives be taken. We have no material weapons, neither spear nor gun, as every one can see.

Non-resistance

Peter Riedemann in his *Confession*, written in 1540 in a Marburg jail, and in other writings, codified Hutterite pacifist beliefs during their most intense period of persecution. At the end of a short sermon—one that is often referred to by Hutterites today—he wrote: 'It is clearly to be seen that one ought neither to avenge himself nor to go to war, but rather offer his back to the strikers, and his cheeks to them that pluck off the hair; that is, suffer with patience and wait upon God, who is righteous, and who will repay it.' The Hutterites believe that they must seek to imitate Christ, that they must cultivate passive obedience, defencelessness, and non-resistance to those who would persecute, kill, or maim them. They are convinced that only in this way can God's love work to bring peace to the world.

Persecution in the U.S.

After nearly 400 years, uncompromising non-resistance was still foremost in Hutterite beliefs and they refused to support the First World War by buying bonds or by joining the army even in a non-combat role. When the United States government called a group of young Hutterite men for military duty, they appeared at the induction centre but refused to sign admission papers, to put on army uniforms, or to take up any kind of duty on the grounds that they were religious objectors to war. Victor Peters writes that there were cases of mock courtmartials at which these conscientious objectors were sentenced to be shot. They were led out to face the firing squad, the countdown was given, and the command to fire—but there were no shots. A reprieve would then be issued to the shocked victims.[15]

Unfortunately for the Hutterites in 1917, their German language reminded Americans that these pacifist strangers were not only refusing to serve the war effort but might actually be helping the enemy What people could not realize, owing to the hysteria of war, was that the Hutterites deliberately retained German to insulate themselves from North American culture.[16] Also, the rigid and formal structure of the German language helped to maintain the order and conformity needed to preserve the Hutterite communal organization that they believed was necessary for full Christian living.

Insidious rumours circulated throughout South Dakota. The Hutterites were accused of salting ground glass in the flour that they milled for public sale. Impetuous fanatics stole Hutterite sheep and cattle from their pastures and, like common thieves, sold them at a fraction of cost to eager buyers. Mobs attacked colonies and some elders were abused and beaten. The Hutterites passively looked on in bewilderment at these actions.

Seventeen hundred Hutterites were but a diminutive minority in the total American population: they had no spokesman or lobby in high places, and their South Dakota lands were far from the centres of power. They were obvious targets because of their separate and distinct way of life and their German ethnic identity. The Hutterians appealed to President Wilson for 'liberty to live according to the dictates of our conscience', while committing themselves to be 'loyal to our God-ordained government and to serve our country in ways which do not interfere with our religious convictions'. But American wartime nationalism seemed to be insulted by the Hutterites' insistence on their divine authority.

The U.S. government tried 503 conscientious objectors for refusing enlistment:[17] 142 received life imprisonment and 17 men were sentenced to death. (No one was executed and all were pardoned by the President shortly after the war.) Of the Hutterites tried, four—Joseph, Michael, and David Hofer, and Jacob Wipf—were sentenced to thirty-seven years in prison for their refusal to enlist.[18] In short order they were confined in the infamous military prison on the island of Alcatraz in San Francisco Bay, where they were handcuffed and at night chained to each other by their ankles. When these men adamantly refused to put on military uniforms, they were thrown into solitary and told that only by complying would they be released from their dungeon. For five days they had the wet, cold, concrete floor for a bed; clad only in their underwear, they endured long hours without food and with only meagre rations of water. At times they were clubbed and tied to the ceiling.

After four months at Alcatraz they were transferred to Fort Leavenworth, Kansas, in chains. From the railway station to the military prison they were prodded with bayonets and herded like oxen through the streets. When they arrived at the prison they were forced to remove their sweat-soaked clothing and to wait for two hours, chilled to the bone, until a prison outfit was given to them. Even then they still had to wait outside in the cold early-morning hours. Joseph and Michael Hofer collapsed and were taken to the hospital. Jacob Wipf and David Hofer were confined to solitary and placed on a starvation diet. They were made to stand nine hours each day, with hands tied and stretched through the prison bars, their feet barely able to touch the floor. Joseph Hofer died in a few days. When his wife came to claim his body, the guards at first would not let her near. Finally, when she was allowed to see the casket, she found that Joseph had been dressed in the uniform that to the end he had refused to wear. Michael Hofer perished a few days later. Within two years most Hutterites had sold or abandoned their colonies, at considerable economic loss, and moved to Canada.[19]

Arrival in Canada

Hutterites view their First World War experience as but one minor episode in their long, harrowing, four-and-a-half-century-old conflict with the world, with governments, and with human nature.[20] As Eli Walter, minister of Spring Creek colony in Montana, put it to an outsider: 'The stronger the pressures are upon us, the stronger we become. In your life you stand alone. In ours there are many to help lift up a fallen brother.'[21] Joseph Kleinsasser, minister of the Lehrerleut colony at Baildon, 15 miles south-east of Moose Jaw, Saskatchewan, added another dimension: 'We stress the risk of persecution and the way of non-violence. We take seriously the day of judgement and believe that our deeds here will be sifted then. We live in common here, but upstairs [in heaven] I can't help you and you can't help me.'

Hutterite elders teach the younger generations to anticipate the possibility of martyrdom at every turn. While nearly every Christian denomination has its saints and heroes, the Anabaptists—and especially the Hutterites—have developed a powerful written tradition of devotional and historical material that vividly portrays the sacrifices made by members of the sect. The *Large Chronicle* of Peter Walpot—the greatest Hutterite missionary organizer of the late sixteenth century—and the *Small Chronicle* of Joannes Waldner (1749-1824)—a zealous convert to the faith—together with the Anabaptist *Martyr's Mirror*, record well over 2,000 eye-witness and other accounts of the martyrdoms of ordinary Anabaptists. Whereas Catholicism has taught in the past that only a few Christians—saints, monks, and nuns—were called by God to the 'perfect life', Hutterites and other Anabaptists teach that all believers are equally saints and ministers of the Gospel and that all are equally accountable for their faith—or lack of it.

For many of the older generation especially, theirs is rarely, in the effervescent North American sense, a joyful life. While the younger families who have lived only in Canada and who have not experienced the traumatic emotional and spiritual upheavals of the past, are more gregarious and exhibit many of the carefree yet restrained traits of Prairie farmers, the elderly cannot forget the persecution of the First World War. Corporal punishment has never befallen Hutterites in Canada, but they have been subject to discriminatory laws and to virulent attacks in the media. Nevertheless Hutterite colonies have multiplied and prospered. This worldly success has incurred the wrath of jealous neighbours and of those who are frightened by a sect that remains anonymous and isolated in communes. The march on Edmonton by Brant and Vulcan area residents, while advertised as a protest against a repeal of the Communal Property Act, was in large part a retaliation against a new Hutterite colony that was being set up in their district—one of eighty-two now in Alberta.[22]

Older Hutterites advise their young to be prepared for the worst from the world. Their chequered history gives them no reason for over-confidence.

NOTES

[1] Member of the Legislative Assembly (MLA) is the term used in most provinces to denote an elected member of the provincial government.

[2] J. W. Eaton and Robert J. Weil, 'The mental health of the Hutterites' in *Scientific American*, vol. 189, no. 6 (Dec. 1953). See also *Culture and mental disorders: a comparative study of Hutterites and other populations* (New York, 1955), by the same authors.

[3] Peter Tschetter, *Hutterian Brethren of yesterday and today* (1966). See also Byran R. Wilson, 'The migrating sects' in the *British journal of sociology*, vol. 18 (Sept. 1967), 303-17.

[4] Hillel Schwartz, 'Early Anabaptist ideas about the nature of children' in *Mennonite quarterly review*, vol. 47 (Apr. 1973), 102ff. 'Anabaptist' was a derogatory term used by sixteenth-century Christians to describe the followers of the many sects that had sprung up and who, despite their divergent beliefs and practices, all rejected the validity of infant baptism.

[5] Paul S. Gross, *The Hutterite way: the inside story of the life, customs, religion and traditions of the Hutterites* (Saskatoon, 1965), p. 39ff., and Robert Friedmann, *Hutterite studies* (Goshen, Ind., 1961), p. 92ff., which analyses the Hutterite doctrine of the 'two worlds'—the religious and the secular. Not all people originally called 'Anabaptist' rejected the alliance between Church and State as the Hutterites, Mennonites, and Amish always have.

[6] Claus-Peter Clasen, *Anabaptism: a social history, 1525-1618* (Ithaca, N.Y., 1973), p. 437, has gathered evidence of 843 known executions of Anabaptists from 1525 to 1618. At least one-half were probably Hutterites.

[7] See John Horsch, *The Hutterian Brethren, 1528-1931, and the principle of non-resistance as held by the Mennonite Church* (Goshen, Ind., 1971). For an unsympathetic historical account of Anabaptism, see A. G. Dickens, *Reformation and society in sixteenth-century Europe* (New York, 1966), p. 125ff.

[8] Clasen, *op. cit.*, p. 244, estimates that the maximum number could well have been 52,200.

[9] Gross, *op. cit.*, pp. 12ff. and 121ff.

[10] By 1878 Mennonites and Amish from Western Europe had been immigrating to North America for over a century. The province of Ontario had a large Anabaptist community in the

Kitchener-Waterloo area that dated back to before 1800. They had been living there without any major difficulties with either government or society.

11 At the census of 1870 the population of Manitoba was 11,963: 558 Indians, 5,757 Métis, 4,083 English half-breeds, and 1,565 Whites. There were 6,247 Roman Catholics and 5,716 Protestants.

12 Norman Thomas, 'The Hutterian Brethren' in *South Dakota historical collections*, vol. 25 (1951), 265-99.

13 British indebtedness to the United States of $2.5 billion, as compared with Germany's debt of $27 million, no doubt encouraged Americans to be more favourable to Great Britain.

14 See Friedmann, *op. cit.*, p. 222ff., and Horsch, *op. cit.*

15 Victor Peters, *All things common: the Hutterian way of life* (Minneapolis, Minn., 1966).

16 Just as the maintenance of German for 100 years in Russia had kept them from absorbing much Russian culture.

17 Hutterites were included among Mennonites, Quakers, and others.

18 For a fuller account of this episode, see John A. Hostetler and Gertrude Enders Huntington, *The Hutterites in North America* (New York, 1967), pp. 9-10.

19 The government of South Dakota spitefully dissolved the Hutterite Church as a corporation. See Thomas, *op. cit.*, and also the Government of Saskatchewan (unpublished) document, *Treatment of the Hutterian Brethren by the provincial and federal governments: a summary* (1963), p. 11.

20 A penetrating insight into the Hutterite attitude can be found in Theron Schlabach (ed.), 'An account by Jakob Waldner: diary of a conscientious objector in World War I', *Mennonite quarterly review*, vol. 47 (Jan. 1974), 73-111.

21 William Albert Allard, 'The Hutterites, plain people of the west' in *National geographic*, vol. 138, no. 1, 112.

22 See George Adolf Mann, 'Functional autonomy among English school teachers in the Hutterite colonies of southern Alberta: a study of social control'. Unpublished Doctor of Philosophy thesis, University of Colorado, 1974, pp. 25 and 270.

Hutterite school children, about 1922.

(Below) During the Spanish-American War of 1898 some Hutterites, fearing they would be conscripted, briefly set up a colony near Dominion City, Manitoba, with the full approval of the Canadian government. At the war's end they sold the land and returned to the U.S.

Welcome to Our City!

From the Calgary Eye-Opener, *September 21, 1918. If the owner and editor, R. A. 'Bob' Edwards, knew the difference between Mennonites and Hutterites, he never let on.*

Hutterite settlers near Winnipeg in the 1920s.

4

ETHNIC CONFLICT: 1914–20

Relatively few Canadians have actually seen Hutterites, much less met and talked with them in person, so successful has the sect been in maintaining its own separate way of life. But this distinct existence (which reflects the Anabaptist belief in the evil and corruptness of the world) has been accomplished at the cost of arousing their neighbours' resentment and dislike. While Hutterites are themselves prejudiced against what they consider to be the unbelief, immorality, and materialism of most outsiders, they have controlled their prejudices by deliberately avoiding society. Many Canadians, on the other hand, have at best treated Hutterites with aloofness and at worst with outright hostility. They express their intolerance openly, and seem to take pleasure in spreading senseless rumours such as 'Hutterite colonies hire men from outside to sire their children' or 'They let their pigs into neighbours' crops' or 'Hutterite boys tamper with machinery left in the fields at night by neighbouring farmers.'

To understand fully the adverse way in which some Canadians have reacted to the Hutterites, it is necessary to explain the environment in which Hutterites found themselves when they came to Manitoba from South Dakota in 1918. At that time Canada was fraught with ethnic distrust and hatred brought about by the First World War.

In the early months of the war the Canadian military effort in Europe was supported by voluntary enlistment—mostly British born. Canadians were optimistic about a short war ('Home for Christmas' was a popular slogan) and the early defeat of Germany

First World War

and her allies. The country soon realized that the ferocity of this war was without precedent in modern history. In the last week of April 1915, 6,000 Canadian soldiers were killed, wounded, or missing in action at the second battle of Ypres. By 1916 one Canadian family in four had a soldier overseas; the average contribution from the towns and cities of Ontario and Manitoba was even higher.

While English Canada accepted the official propaganda that the war was a world struggle for democracy, freedom, and liberty, French Canada, which was traditionally loyal above all else to family, province, and religion, had come to see the war as a 'British' problem, an imperial conflict between two global giants, Germany and Great Britain, who had dragged their helpless colonies into battle without care or concern for their welfare. The English-language press began to attack the French-speaking Canadians with statistics to show that their army enlistment rates were abysmally low and demanded that they do their share of the fighting.

Conscription The Conservative federal government under Prime Minister Robert Borden became convinced that to maintain Canada's strength and responsibility in the war, conscription was absolutely necessary. Preparations were made to draw up a Military Service Bill. The government realized, however, that compulsory military service would split the country and cost the Conservative Party its power, so negotiations were begun with Liberals sympathetic to conscription. The formation of a coalition was suggested to see the war through to a quick and successful conclusion.

The conscription bill was introduced in the House of Commons in May 1917—none too soon for those who wanted the war effort expanded; during April and May there were 20,000 Canadian war casualties but only 3,000 enlistments. When the Military Service Act was passed on August 17, twenty English-speaking Liberals supported it and Sir Wilfrid Laurier's opposition party seemed on the verge of dismemberment. He could not vote for conscription, no matter how strongly he felt about British democracy, because he had guaranteed his fellow French-speaking Canadians, when he pleaded for their all-out war effort in previous years, that the country would never implement compulsory military duty. He would not resign as party leader because to do so would be to desert the leadership of French Canadians. He feared the possibility of Quebec extremists' taking over and leading the province out of Confederation. In his mind national unity came before the war. But many Liberal MPs and the majority of the English-speaking party membership were adamant that every Canadian should participate fully in the war. In October 1917 these Liberals entered into a coalition with Borden and the Conservatives. The Union Government was formed to implement conscription and to fight the approaching federal election (December 17, 1917) that was made necessary because the legal term of Parliament was about to expire.

Borden's government had wanted to ensure that it would not lose this election and in the late summer, before the coalition, it had passed the Wartime Elections Act to lessen opposition. It thereby enshrined itself as the most undemocratic Parliament in Canada's history. By this act the right to vote was given to Canadian women for the first time, but not to all women or even to those who were doing war work in factories or on farms—only to those who were related to soldiers. The Act also allowed soldiers to vote in any constituency in Canada they wished. (At election time sergeant majors were instructed to tell their men to vote in those ridings in which a majority of the Union Government was in doubt.) Worst of all, the right to vote was taken away from conscientious objectors and from immigrants who had been naturalized as Canadians (i.e. Canadian citizens of 'alien' birth). The author of these two acts, Arthur Meighen—the member from Portage La Prairie, Manitoba, and Solicitor-General—said in the House of Commons on September 6, 1917:

This bill disqualifies for the War Time Election those of alien enemy birth or other European birth and of alien enemy mother tongue or native language, who have been naturalized since the thirty-first of March, 1902. It is further to be noted that whosoever is disqualified from voting by this measure is at the same time exempted from combatant service in the war.

The term 'alien enemy'[1] seemed coined to slander those who sought

Wartime Elections Act

freedom in Canada from European militarism before the war and who would most likely now be pacifist, anti-conscriptionist, or Liberal Party supporters. Thus the war that was to 'save democracy' caused democracy to be threatened in Canada itself.

1917 Election

The early-winter election was perhaps the bitterest in Canadian history, fought as it was amid the continued slaughter of Canadians in Europe, the divisive question of conscription, and the alienation of French from English. The non-coalition Liberals ensured that Unionist candidates were howled down in every public meeting they attempted to hold in the province of Quebec— the Prime Minister did not dare to campaign in Montreal for fear of violence—and there was actual rioting and gunfire in Quebec City. 'A vote for Laurier is a vote for the Kaiser,' proclaimed Unionist propaganda with vehemence. However, the Union Government was overwhelmingly elected and received a majority of 71 seats. All but 20 seats[2] across the country went Union—except in Quebec, where Laurier and his Liberals won 62 out of 65.

Manitoba

The war cultivated an extreme national self-consciousness and brought home to English-speaking Canadians the fact that there was not one uniform cultural identity throughout the country. Manitoba, which already had a longstanding French-English division, had only recently become aware that the vast immigration from Europe before the war (almost a million immigrants had come to the Prairies in the previous twenty years) had produced a heterogeneous province with, among many other peoples, large Icelandic, Mennonite, and Ukrainian communities. The Winnipeg *Free Press*—the most respected and prominent daily newspaper in Manitoba[3]—was deeply perturbed that only fifty-eight per cent of Manitoba's population was of British descent. It reported on September 6, 1918 that 273,218 of the total Prairie population of 1,698,220 was of 'enemy alien origin', by which it meant people from Germany and Austro-Hungary.

The presence of these unassimilated people made many citizens very uncomfortable. There was little doubt in their minds that the retention of the religious beliefs, values, language, and customs of minorities must be secondary to national unity. They believed that only by uniform thought and behaviour could Canadians produce the strength necessary for success in the life-and-death struggle against Germany, Austro-Hungary, and Turkey. If Canada was to be a great nation, observed the Lethbridge *Herald*, then a Canadian must think 'enough of Canada to sacrifice his life, if it need be, for it'. Indeed most early-twentieth-century Canadians assumed that democracy was dependent upon the quick assimilation of immigrants and their conformity to English-Canadian ways. Even J. S. Woodsworth—former Methodist minister, pacifist, and future founder and influential leader of the CCF Party[4]—who devoted several years of his life to helping immigrants in Winnipeg, had written of their closely knit communities:

Isolated from Canadian people, they are much slower to enter upon Canadian life. Such colonies are really bits of Russia or Austria or Germany transplanted to Canada. Not only are they less open to Canadian ideas, but closely united, they can control the entire community. The social, the educational, the religious, the political life is dominated by alien ideas.[5]

The *Free Press* called the Mennonites of Manitoba—German-speaking Anabaptists, like the Hutterites, who had also fled from Russia in the 1870s and were still unassimilated—'dirty shirkers' for their pacifist convictions and 'aliens' because of their German cultural and linguistic background. 'If this country is not good enough to fight for,' the newspaper declared, 'it is not good enough to live in.'

A favourite target of liberal nationalists in their drive to assimilate foreigners was the system of bilingual public schools that had been established in Manitoba in 1897. While English was expected to be the normal language of instruction in all schools, French or foreign-language schools could be given public monies if there were at least ten pupils in attendance whose mother tongue was not English. This seemed to be a reasonable political compromise between the French- and English-speaking national groups because in 1897 the only other minority of any size were Mennonites, but they already had private schools, which were conducted in German.[6]

After 1897, however, a large influx of East-European immigrants flooded into Manitoba. Every ethnic area could legally have a teacher of its own nationality (and religious persuasion). But as most peasant groups did not have enough competent teachers for their own language, much less to teach English as well, there were, in 110 school districts, one or more ethnic minorities that had to send their children to schools that were taught in the language of another minority. German Lutherans might have to attend Roman Catholic Polish schools, or Orthodox Ukrainians those of Protestant Icelanders. The wartime hysteria over 'enemy aliens' and the lack of national unity made the English-speaking community determined to end this mix-up and finally to establish, in and through the public-school system, English as the language and British as the culture of all Manitobans.

In 1914 the Manitoba Liberal Party (which was dominated by Clifford Sifton, the powerful owner of the Winnipeg *Free Press*) adopted a nationalistic political platform aimed directly at the assimilation of minority groups. It served notice that, if elected, it would implement a new nationalism through a province-wide school system, compulsory school attendance, and obligatory use of English as the language of instruction. The propaganda arm of the party, the *Free Press*, carried the program to the community.

In the public school system and in the maintenance of a common language in equal opportunity for all our children, no matter where their origin, and in the abolition of everything which serves to perpetuate racial difference, lies the hope of our nation.

Bilingual schools were abolished in 1916 by the newly elected Liberal government of Manitoba under the premiership of T. C. Norris. Schooling was made compulsory for all children aged seven to fourteen. During the war only the worst infractions were dealt with, and it was not until the fall of 1918, partially through the continual goading of the *Free Press*, that steps were taken by the government to force the 20,000 Mennonites and other recalcitrant minorities to obey the school laws. The government began to enforce the 1916 regulations in 1918, without any consideration of the fact that all but the most conservative Mennonite schools had been based on a sincere and competent educational system in which pupils learned to read, write, and speak both German and English. There were many cases where parents, as conscientious objectors to laws they considered unjust, were fined or jailed for not sending their children to a government-approved school. One-third of Manitoba Mennonites—the group that equated speaking English with speedy assimilation and loss of religious belief—eventually left Canada during the twenties to seek religious freedom in Latin America.

While the Mennonites of Manitoba were being arrested and tried for their disobedience to provincial law, the Hutterites began to arrive and settle in the province. Though they came at the *invitation of the federal government*, in the mind of the unknowing public they were Mennonites and they received equal scorn and abuse.[7]

Before they moved to Canada in 1918 the Hutterites were assured by the Canadian government that they would be accorded the same privileges previously granted to the Mennonites in 1873: complete military exemption, the right to independent private schools, and permission to settle communally.[8] Hostile Prairie newspapers immediately set out to whip up contrary public opinion—the war conveniently provided many excuses. On September 9, 1918, the *Free Press*, its wartime nationalistic fervour stung by the presence in Manitoba of thousands of Mennonites of pacifist disposition, noted that, for the Hutterites,

there must be no special privileges of any kind. We see no reason why non-English immigrants should not be required, as precedent to admission, to subscribe to a declaration which will leave them in no doubt as to what will be expected of them. That declaration should include a specific recognition of the obligation to bear arms if called upon by the authorities. We want no more 'non-resisters' and conscientious objectors to military service.

At times the *Free Press* seemed to despair over the destiny of Canadians—i.e. Anglo-Saxons—and over whether they could fight off the hordes of immigrants who threatened their cultural supremacy. Several days later the newspaper was saying, 'All alien immigration should be stopped until after the war,' and it went on to make the most common charge of all against the Hutterites: that they, and other immigrants, were 'land-grabbers'.

Already Canadians are being driven out from many of the finest districts in Canada by the immense congregating together of foreign elements. Who and what are these hordes of aliens coming to the west now from across the United States border? Do we know or care?[9]

The land occupied by the Hutterites was very far from being the finest in Canada. While those Canadians who were glad to sell to the newcomers escaped criticism, the purchasers were treated as a menace. They were never interviewed; their critics wrote about them emotionally from a distance, not from first-hand experience.

Alberta Twice as many Hutterites entered Alberta as Manitoba and there the reaction was just as severe and widespread. Three colonies were established in the Calgary area and nine close to Lethbridge. Anti-pacifist, anti-German, and pro-assimilation spokesmen cried out against these strangely dressed, shy exiles from American persecution. Throughout September and October 1918 notorious 'Bob' Edwards, in his popular and widely read Calgary *Eye-Opener*, showed a remarkable propensity for misinformation and prejudice. He referred to the Hutterites as 'Mennonite slackers'. 'God knows how many are coming here from the States, but it is said the particular brotherhood which has been wished on Alberta has two million members . . . who are coming to Canada.'[10] He decried 'this bunch of eccentrics who refuse to fight for the country they make their home in'; they 'should have been shoo'd back at the line. They are undesirables.' Inflammatory phrases came easily to Edwards and, in denigrating the Hutterites' desire to retain their German language, he spoke of German as the 'language of the father-land'—an expression well calculated to stir up the antagonistic emotions of wartime. In bold type the *Eye-Opener* screamed, 'BUT WHY DO THEY WANT TO IMPOSE SUCH A BUNCH OF GERMAN CATTLE ON US? THAT GETS OUR GOAT. WHY?'

Newspapers found an eager audience for these sentiments among individuals who might normally have kept a personal check on prejudice in their everyday attitudes and dealings with others.

But intolerance becomes acceptable in wartime. In the First World War it was shared openly by a large number of citizens and was publicly demonstrated particularly in an avid but narrow British nationalism (which grew up to counterbalance French-speaking pacifism) that supported the war effort and backed the Union Government and conscription. This trauma revealed a national insecurity, a feeling of mass inadequacy and helplessness, and fear of the future—the favourite scapegoats being foreign-language groups. The cultural distinctiveness of the Hutterites' dress and communalism, their hated German language and pacifism, and their unfamiliar religion made them highly suspect.

This persecution of minority groups and the demand for their assimilation also originated in two cultural attitudes that pervaded North American society. Once the liberal democratic principle of majority rule became accepted in the English-speaking world in the late nineteenth century, and small privileged aristocratic classes were forced to give up power to elected legislatures that were responsible to the will of the majority of the people, any minority had to accept majority decisions quietly. When this principle was established in government, it became almost axiomatic in all social matters as well and led, during the First World War, to a social tyranny in Canada. Canadians could not understand why immigrants who chose to come to Canada would not accept the responsibilities of democratic citizenship such as military duty. There was no precedent in an egalitarian society for anything but conformity; all citizens must be equal. The majority dictated that there must be no conscientious objectors, and those who persisted in being different must be assimilated or face intimidation and persecution.

Conformity

The other cultural attitude behind the Canadian desire to assimilate minority groups stemmed from the formidable influence that Charles Darwin's *Origin of Species* (1859) had exerted in the development of nineteenth-century social science in the English-speaking world and in Western Europe. The Darwinian concept of 'survival of the fittest', while only a theory, and a biological one at that, was eagerly appropriated by anthropologists and other scholars who were beginning to apply the methods and insights of

Social Darwinism

natural science to the study of socio-cultural groups and human behaviour (i.e. 'Social Darwinism'). Anthropologists theorized that peoples of the world could be classified into racial groups (by 1900 five were usually accepted: Caucasian, Mongolian, Malayan, Negro, and American Indian), and that empirical evidence proved that the fairer-skinned race of the Northern hemisphere—the 'Nordic' race—was the normal race from which all others had deviated. Whites were superior, more intelligent, and more beautiful; they were also technologically more advanced, more fit to survive and, therefore, superior to the darker-skinned races (including the 'whites' of Eastern Europe). Many whites actually became fearful that intermarriage, and mixing with these 'inferior' peoples, would contaminate their race.

Canadians easily accepted the attitude of superiority towards 'lesser races' that now became commonplace. On the other hand, they also accepted a new spirit in western-world churches called the 'Social Gospel', which moved many ministers and lay people in Canada to become interested in the immigrant and his problems. While accepting the Social Darwinian concepts of racial inferiority, they believed that as Christians they were duty bound to try to raise up the lower races—that is, the immigrants—from their 'inferiority'.

Social Gospel

James Shaver Woodsworth (1874-1942) was one of Canada's earliest Social Gospelers and eventually the best known. Although he began his career in the Methodist ministry, riding on horseback through rural southern Manitoba, a stint of post-graduate study in England put him in touch with the Social Gospel. By 1907 he had committed himself to social-service work with immigrants at the Methodist All People's Mission in the crowded tenement district of Winnipeg's North End. High on Woodsworth's priority list was the implementation of free government-controlled compulsory schooling that would give immigrant children knowledge and understanding to overcome their poverty and ignorance. Woodsworth joined the growing chorus of voices that demanded of the Manitoba government that it take more initiative in schooling the immigrants in Canadian ways. While he was advocating their assimilation, he was also quick to lash out at his fellow Canadians who wouldn't take time to understand these newcomers. Unconscious of his own Social Darwinist racial bias, he stated that

we must divest ourselves of a certain arrogant superiority and exclusiveness, perhaps characteristic of the English race. Our untravelled Canadian despises all foreigners alike . . . We must learn that the world is wide, and that there are a great many other types than our own, and some just as good, though different.[11]

The war wiped out the efforts of the Social Gospelers to make citizens more aware of, and sympathetic to, immigrants and their problems. Where immigrants were concerned, public sentiment soon turned to mistrust and sometimes to hate. Even the Methodist Church, which had contributed heavily to the Social Gospel movement, became caught up in the egalitarian idea of individual sacrifice for the common national good. The Methodists adopted the war as a holy crusade for Christianity—'a redemptive war'—in which true believers were to 'catch the martyr spirit' and give 'sacrificial duty'. Hundreds of Methodist ministers served in the army—ninety per cent in a combatant role. Those who stayed home recruited for the army from their pulpits and supported the Union Government and conscription in their sermons. In appreciation of Methodist nationalism, the federal government amazingly and obtusely hired an English-speaking Protestant (the Reverend C. A. Williams) to take charge of army recruiting in the province of Quebec.[12]

The Church gave whole-hearted endorsement to the Wartime Elections Act, such was its patriotism and its feeling against conscientious objectors, many of whom were foreign born. There was little sympathy for minorities and little tolerance for those who seemed to be asking for privileges while others were giving their lives. The Methodist *Christian Guardian* summed up the anti-pacifist feeling of most Canadian liberal democrats who believed in majority rule:

We may not feel like forcing such a man to fight, nor like punishing him for his honest opinions; but if he is honest, then let him be prepared to take the full consequence of his opinions. If he does not believe it is right to fight in defence of his privileges as a citizen, then . . . such a man would have no legal rights. He could not vote, he could not hold property, he could not in case of invasion of his rights call upon the Government or the courts for protection.[13]

The *Guardian* later took a strong stand against anti-war church groups. 'In the time of war', the paper proclaimed, 'any type of religion which is pro-German is not a desirable type for this country, and any type which is not ardently pro-British and pro-American is not very much better.'

Since even the Methodists, regarded as the most socially progressive pre-war Church, were alienated from immigrants and pacifists, it is easy to see why Hutterites felt intimidated by Canadian hostility in 1918. There seemed to be no one willing to speak out except in opposition to them.

Control of immigration

The Calgary *Eye-Opener* perceptively forecast that, when the war was over, returning veterans would be more resentful of the Hutterites than of any other group of Albertans. The paper categorically declared that 'the returned soldiers and citizens generally will not stand' for Hutterite exemption from military service. 'It is too much to expect of a people who have so loyally contributed their best blood to the overseas army.' Correctly, the newspaper predicted that future strife would revolve around the claims that war veterans were unable to compete with the well-organized and efficient Hutterites in purchasing good land, which was in short supply.

Their colonies require large blocks of land . . . and these are exactly what the returned soldier must have if the great problem of demobilization is to be solved . . . It is maddening to think that just at the time when Soldier Land Settlement problems are presenting so many difficulties in the way of finding suitable lands accessible to railways and civilization, then hordes of Mennonites[14] *are allowed to flock into Canada from the States in order to escape military service.*

When the Hutterites arrived in Canada in September 1918, agitation against them, and against other pacifists, made itself felt in public statements, petitions, and telegrams to government offi-

cials and elected representatives.[15] Not only did groups like the
Great War Veterans Association and the Great War Next of Kin
Association, from towns and cities in southern Alberta and Mani-
toba, complain about the privileges of the Hutterites, but they
demanded that foreign immigration be stopped and that any
exemptions given immigrant groups be immediately rescinded.
The veterans found an ally in the Board of Home Missions and
Social Service of the Presbyterian Church, which publicly stated its

*disapproval of the policy of permitting large numbers of persons
of foreign language and tradition to settle in contiguity so that the
process of assimilation becomes unduly slow and the growth of
the proper national spirit is retarded.*

Furthermore the Board supported the anti-pacifist and pro-Anglo-
phone opinion

*that all persons entering the country as settlers should be prepared
to undertake their fair share of all national burdens, including
national defense, and the strongest discouragement should be
given to the instituting of schools in which work is carried on in
the German or other foreign language.*

Violent opposition to the Hutterites became focused in Parliament, particularly in the outspoken attacks of Members from
Alberta. William Ashbury Buchanan, a Liberal-Unionist MP for
Lethbridge, reminded the vote-conscious Members that not only
returned soldiers but many other citizens were upset as well.

*A number of Canadian clubs throughout Western Canada have
declared themselves against the entrance of these people [Hutter-
ites] into the Dominion. Now the Canadian clubs, as I know them,
are supposed to represent a very high type of citizenship; they want
to perpetuate the very best ideals of our citizenship, and if after
mature consideration by men of all parties and of all creeds, the
Canadian clubs in Winnipeg and elsewhere in the West declare
that it is not in the interest of Canada that these people should be
allowed to settle in this country . . .*[16]

The federal government gave in to public pressure and issued

Orders-in-Council revoking the military exemption that was guaranteed to Hutterites in 1899 (April 1919) and prohibited further immigration of South Dakota Hutterites (May and June 1919).[17] To the public the government gave this explanation:

Owing to conditions prevailing as a result of war, a widespread feeling exists throughout Canada . . . that steps should be taken to prohibit the landing in Canada of immigrants deemed undesirable owing to their particular customs, habits, modes of living, and methods of holding property, and because of their probable inability to become readily assimilated . . .[18]

In a letter of September 1919 to Hutterite Joseph Kleinsasser, Milltown, South Dakota, the Hon. J. A. Calder, Minister of Immigration, wrote in similar fashion, but concluded:

If, in the future, this decision should be reversed, it will depend largely, if not entirely, upon the conduct and mode of life of those of your people now settled in Canada. Unless they are prepared to become Canadian citizens in the truest and best sense of the term, and . . . assume all the obligations of citizenship including military service, it is extremely doubtful if any government in Canada would be prepared to admit them.

The betrayal of the Hutterites who were already in Canada and the infidelity of the Canadian government towards the groups still in South Dakota can partly be rationalized by the fact that the wartime coalition Union Government underwent immense stress and pressures in the early post-war months. There was rapid inflation and increased unemployment as factories producing war materials closed and returning soldiers could not find jobs. Workers had seen war profiteers use the holocaust for their own benefit[19] and now, with discontented soldiers, they gathered together in Calgary, in March 1919, to form the One Big Union—a super-union patterned on a similar American organization. The OBU drew up a constitution with these introductory words—somewhat reminiscent of Karl Marx: 'Modern industrial society is divided into two classes, those who possess and do not produce and those who produce and do not possess. Between these two classes a continual struggle takes place.'

The Canadian government feared that a Bolshevik takeover, such as had occurred in Russia, was near at hand. The OBU seemed the first step in the direction of a workers' revolution. Resolutions of the OBU passed at the Calgary conference called for the complete abolition of private property and, because the Canadian system of parliamentary government was a 'capitalistic device to crush the legitimate aspirations of labour', for the establishment of workers' soviets (elected councils). The subsequent Winnipeg General Strike—from May 15 to June 26, 1919—seemed to the confused federal and local authorities to be the first step towards civil violence and rebellion.

The *Free Press* gave its prejudiced interpretation of the strike and its extremist solution of future labour problems.

The idea . . . is to employ these masses of rough, uneducated foreigners, who know nothing of our customs and our civilization, to browbeat and override the intelligent and skilled craftsmen of the more technical trades who are numerically weaker. The surest way to break the hold of the anarchist . . . upon labour is to clean the aliens out of the community.[20]

The Victoria *Daily Times* said of the strike that 'it might not be very surprising to find that Bolshevik pedagogues were at the back of the whole business'. The Slavic peoples of Eastern Europe were particularly suspect because of their supposed 'racial' affinities with the peoples of the Soviet Union. *La Presse* was also alarmist in May 1919: 'There is no longer any doubt about it. Bolshevism has for certain planted its tent at Winnipeg. There exists . . . a worker's news-sheet that claims the striker's aim to found a government of Soviets, as there is in Russia.'

The federal government reacted to the anti-alien propaganda by amending the Immigration Act on June 6 to permit the deportation, without trial, of any person who was not a British subject. The victims of this action were to include any person who was even 'suspected of belonging to any secret society or organization . . . or who was a member of or affiliated with any organization entertaining or teaching disbelief in or opposition to organized government.' While this Act was not used to deport any Hutterites, it showed that discriminatory legislation against pacifists was only one aspect of the hysteria against foreigners in 1919.

As a tiny, non-violent, pacifist religious sect, the Hutterites could no more than cower before the onslaught of public displeasure at the federal government's decision to allow them into Canada in 1918, and they could do nothing about the government's reversal of policy the next year. They would not use the newspapers or the courts to defend themselves from intolerance and prejudice because, in fact, they expected no better treatment—such had been their chequered history of persecution during the previous 400 years.[21] Whenever they had managed to thrive and prosper, wars had swept the land and persecution had driven them to seek peace and new homes elsewhere.

The Winnipeg General Strike fizzled out after six weeks; within a year or so wartime anti-foreign feeling subsided and the Union Government disintegrated as party politics regained its former adherents. In the general election of 1921 William Lyon Mackenzie King, the new Liberal Party leader, promised his constituency in Waterloo, Ontario, where there was a large Mennonite population, that if he was elected and became Prime Minister he would repeal the order restricting immigration, which he did in 1922. Many of the Hutterites who had been forced by the 1919 ban to remain behind in South Dakota—at great hardship for separated families—were now able to come to Canada. Only three colonies remained in South Dakota.

During the twenties, King's Liberal government tried to build a nation independent of Britain and to reconstruct the national unity that had been destroyed by wartime nationalism. Prosperity and security returned and, in the relative affluence of the decade, the Hutterites were left alone to build up their colonies and to grow in number.

NOTES

[1] By 'alien enemy' they meant Germans and Austrians, but also, because of language, Czechs, Slovaks, Poles, Ukrainians, Swiss, and Russians who spoke a Germanic dialect. Mennonites, Hutterites, and Doukhobors were specifically named in sub-section 154 as being excluded from voting.

[2] Two ridings in western Canada, eight in Ontario, and ten in the Maritimes elected Liberals.

[3] The *Free Press* was a bold crusader for the goals of Sir Clifford Sifton, its ambitious owner who was also a federal MP, and of its indomitable editor, John W. Dafoe—both staunch Liberals.

[4] The Co-operative Commonwealth Federation was established in 1935 and today is known as the New Democratic Party.

[5] See also J. S. Woodsworth, *Strangers within our gates* (1909; reprinted Toronto, 1972), p. 234; and J. E. Rea, 'The roots of Prairie society' in David P. Gagan (ed.), *Prairie perspectives: papers of the Western Canadian Studies Conference* (Toronto, 1970), pp. 46-55.

[6] By virtue of their agreement with the federal government, made when they entered Canada in the 1970s.

[7] The federal government's action in inviting the South Dakota Hutterites to come to Canada was paradoxical. It had passed discriminatory legislation against pacifists in the Wartime Elections Act, yet it allowed more of them into the country! The proven agricultural abilities of the Hutterites no doubt played a large part in giving them entry at a time when farm labour was in short supply and food was vitally needed.

[8] Further information on agreements made between the Hutterites and the Canadian government can be found in A. M. Willms, 'The brethren known as Hutterians' in *Canadian journal of economics and political science*, vol. 24 (1958), 391ff., and in Edwin A. Pitt, 'The Hutterite Brethren in Alberta' (1949), an unpublished M.A. thesis for the University of Alberta.

[9] Winnipeg *Free Press*, Sept. 13, 1918.

[10] 1,700 actually came. Alberta's population was 588,454 in 1921.

[11] J. S. Woodsworth, *op. cit.*, p. 240.

12 Perhaps the government was convinced that most volunteers would be English-speaking in any case.

13 This editorial caused pacifist J. S. Woodsworth to resign from the Methodist ministry.

14 The newspaper couldn't (or wouldn't) distinguish between Mennonites and Hutterites.

15 For a description and analysis of Canadian reaction to Hutterites, see Howard Palmer, 'The Hutterite land expansion controversy in Alberta' in *Western Canada journal of anthropology* (July 1971), 18-46, and his chapter on Hutterites in *Land of the second chance* (Lethbridge, 1972).

16 Quoted by Frank H. Epp in 'Canada and the American draft-dodger in World War I', a paper prepared for the 51st annual meeting of the Canadian Historical Association (Montreal, 1972), p. 13.

17 And Mennonite and Doukhobor immigration as well.

18 Quoted by Palmer, *op. cit.*, 22.

19 25,000 MacAdam shovels, the patent for which was held by the secretary of the Minister of Militia, were supplied to the troops at a cost of $1.35 each and were to act as an entrenching tool. The ³⁄₁₆-inch blade was also intended to shield the soldier against enemy bullets from 300 yards. Found useless for both purposes, they were eventually sold for scrap metal. Further discussion on other wartime scandals and profiteering may be found in Jack Blyth, 'Emerging Canadian independence: Canadians and the Great War' in *The quarterly of Canadian studies for the secondary school* , vol. 3, no. 2 (1974).

20 Winnipeg *Free Press*, May 23, 1919.

21 In later years the Hutterites did use the courts. See page 115.

(Right) The colony machine-shop must have parts for every eventuality. Usually they are bought in bulk from urban suppliers.

Part Three

THE HUTTERITES IN A
TECHNOLOGICAL AGE

(Above) On-the-spot education of one generation by another—a scene in the machine-shop.

(Left) A modern technological farm relies on workable machinery for peak periods of operation like seed-time and harvest. On every colony one Hutterite at least must be a skilled mechanic.

Large quantities of meat are kept in cold storage.

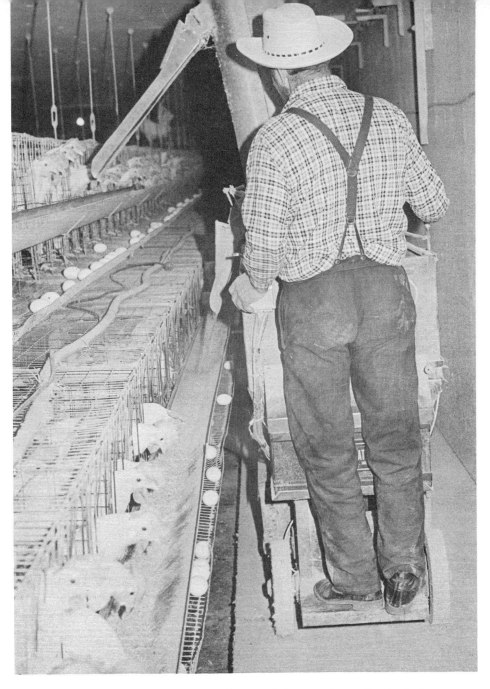

Egg production utilizes nearly every labour-saving technological advance. Thousands of hens are fed from a machine on which the operator can ride down the lengthy aisles of the hen house.

A tractor cultivating a field with a discer.

This modern tractor has a cab that is enclosed and may be air-conditioned as well to protect the 'field man', not only from wind and rain but from dust and chaff. Being able to keep up with the latest farm machinery and technology is a challenge to all who farm large acreages on the Prairies.

A typical farming region in the foothills of the Rockies.

5

ECONOMIC CONFLICT: 1920–74

After the First World War, in the twenties and thirties, there was still a residue of racial and ethnic hatred in Canada. Stalinist terror campaigns against minorities in the Soviet Union caused 20,000 German-speaking Mennonites to flee to Canada to escape torture, imprisonment, exile to Siberia, and forced assimilation. Many of these refugees settled in Prairie areas where there were already large concentrations of Hutterites and Mennonites. The Board of Trade of Southern Alberta became alarmed and in 1927 began to protest against the Mennonites and Hutterites who, it claimed, were the 'wrong kind of settlers' and were acquiring the 'best' lands. 'If we cannot obtain British and good northern European settlers,' warned the Board in a press release that expressed the Social Darwinian outlook, 'it would be better to have no immigrants at all.' Under public pressure the Canadian government closed the door on immigration in 1929 and stopped the new wave of Mennonites from reaching Canada. However, a small number of Dakota Hutterites were admitted in 1931.[1]

Pressures to assimilate

In the late summer of that year the Wolf Creek colony of South Dakota made plans to move to southern Alberta. But the party of Premier J. E. Brownlee—the United Farmers of Alberta—was determined to keep them out. 'We regret to have to say that these people have not proven very satisfactory immigrants,' Brownlee remarked to the federal Minister of Immigration. 'We quite admit that they are frugal, industrious, and hard working, but on the other hand they do not assimilate or mix with other people in the province.' Assimilation was still a touchy political issue and the government wished to keep tempers down and to maintain harmony in the province.

Brownlee was joined by provincial legislators and boards of trade in the New Dayton and Warner areas to pressure the federal government to halt the move. However, when lawyers hired by the Hutterites were able to show Ottawa that the prospective immigrants had already sold their Dakota land and had made binding financial commitments in Canada, the Conservative government refused to disallow the Hutterites' entry. The government of Alberta finally agreed, reluctantly, to accept the Hutterites in August 1931 after it had been approached by the Hutterites' lawyers, the federal immigration department, the colonization board of the CPR, and the Lethbridge Board of Trade.

Two months later the Hutterites negotiated entry for another group of their people to join a colony at Magrath, Alberta.[2] The provincial government responded to this by claiming that there had been a gentleman's agreement to the effect that additional members of the sect would not come into the province, that all colonies would be incorporated, and that landholdings would not be increased. The Hutterites denied the existence of this agreement. The group intended for Magrath were allowed entry only when the federal immigration department again intervened.

The first Hutterite immigrants to Alberta sent their children to nearby one-room schoolhouses. However, farming families did not like their children mixing with Hutterite youngsters, and community pressure resulted in the Hutterites' establishing and maintaining, at their own expense, a school on each colony. The provincial government and the local school board have kept up this arrangement and the Hutterites continue to pay school taxes in return for qualified teachers. There are still no Hutterite children in Canada attending schools outside their colonies.[3]

In 1931 Edwin A. Pitt, an elementary school teacher at Daly Creek, Alberta, was asked by a delegation from the local Hutterite colony if he would be willing to teach sixteen of their children at his school. The Depression had so affected their finances that they were having difficulty maintaining their own school. The prevailing attitude was revealed in what he said to them. Though Pitt claimed to be sympathetic to the Hutterites, his attitude was condescending and he showed a complete lack of understanding of the Hutterites' religion:

Personally I am glad to welcome these Hutterite children into my school. I know of no better way to make Canadians out of them. I have not the least doubt that, through association with our own boys and girls, through observation of our ways, our customs and our manner of dress, and by taking part in our games and by learning our songs, they will become quite dissatisfied with the colourless, monotonous life of the colony. These children will be quick to learn and to adopt our way of life, and to discard that which circumstance and accident of birth now forces upon them. It is through the children that we will break up these colonies, these islands of isolation within our midst, and eventually bring about a true assimilation of the Hutterites into Alberta and Canadian society.[4]

The delegation quietly walked out of the meeting and never again returned or asked to send their children to that public school.

Pitt later made friends with Hutterites and researched their history and beliefs. One Hutterite chanced to ask him why they were not liked better by their neighbours. Pitt suggested that they should take more part in community life and, perhaps, help to build the skating rink that the district needed and wanted.

The good man's answer, in itself a question, was rather staggering: 'Tell me', he said, 'did Jesus Christ ever skate?' To my perplexed reply that Christ had lived in a land where ice seldom existed, he answered, 'Any departure from the old way is bad; one thing soon leads to another.'[5]

Today Hutterite youngsters do skate on Prairie ponds and they enjoy zipping across the ice on homemade skate boards. *But they do not play hockey.*

Depression   World finances were in chaos during the 'dirty thirties'. Money stopped circulating, mass unemployment spread, and those countries that could produce food found their markets shrivelling as prices dropped lower and lower. Nowhere was the Depression felt so badly as on the farms of the short, coarse-grass regions of south-eastern Alberta (and south-western Saskatchewan)—a dustbowl area known as the 'Palliser Triangle'. A few years of drought and high winds during the early 1930s eroded the shallow topsoil of this treeless, barren country and brought almost total crop failure to those farmers who, in the optimistic spirit of western settlement in the early 1900s, had mortgaged themselves heavily to buy the last available cheap land in the southern Prairie provinces.

Wheat prices in Canada fell from $1.60 a bushel in 1929 to 38¢ a bushel by the end of 1932, the same year that thousand-pound choice steers were practically given away in Calgary for $22.50.[6] In a vain attempt to keep prices up, farmers burned or dumped wheat and other foodstuffs, but to no avail.[7] Those Prairie farmers who managed to harvest a crop hardly recovered production costs, and the unfortunates of the Palliser Triangle often had no harvest at all. Thousands of people could not afford to buy food and were forced to go to bed hungry or to stand in long lines for charitable handouts. When faced with large welfare rolls—$15 a month per family plus a small clothing allowance—many of the municipal governments of southern Alberta faced bankruptcy and frantically looked for a way out of their predicament.

They found a kind of salvation in the Hutterites. These communal people, who had built a reputation for self-sufficiency, had made a policy of doing without rather than calling on governments for help. Moreover, there were Hutterites in South Dakota who could afford to buy out those farmers who couldn't meet their mortgage payments. They would displace the welfare cases and farm the land more efficiently.[8] In a complete reversal of attitude, municipal councils and business groups from depressed areas like Milk River, Raymond, Warner, Cardston, and Lethbridge in 1934 pressured both the federal and provincial governments to admit still more Hutterites.

The government of Alberta was itself close to bankruptcy and welcomed any means of improving its finances and those of its local governments. Premier Brownlee, hitherto a foe of the Hutterites, now had a sanguine view of further Hutterite immigration. The Hutterites were able to survive the Depression better than individual farmers because of the co-operation between colonies, the diversity of their farm operation, and their simple style of living. By 1935 even South Dakota decided it wanted to keep its one remaining Hutterite colony and again passed a law allowing colonies to incorporate.[9] Everyone now wanted the Hutterites.

Second World War

In 1939 the Second World War broke out and Canada was once more embroiled in conflict with Germany. With the economy starting to boom, Prairie newspapers, civic organizations, and patriotic leagues all joined in reviving the debate that had accompanied the entry of Hutterites into Canada in 1918-19. This time hostility was directed at their continued rapid land expansion while other farmers were fighting a war that the Hutterites preferred to ignore.[10] Some, like the Loyalist League at Pincher Creek, wanted the sect expelled from the country, their property confiscated, and their land resold, cheaply, to assimilable Canadians. Others, like the Alberta chapter of the I.O.D.E. and the United Farmers of Alberta (now out of power), wanted the repeal of the federal guarantee of Hutterite military exemption.

At first many Hutterites stoutly maintained their traditional non-violent convictions: they refused military duty and alternative service as well. On this account several were jailed for short periods.[11] Eventually, however, they (along with Mennonites, Doukhobors, and Quakers, et al.) considerably compromised their First World War stand and accepted placement in labour camps for road work and forestry duty. As one Hutterite woman put it, 'Better to feed bears in the parks than to kill people.' The government allowed a Hutterite minister in each camp to help the conscripted youth keep their communal rules and discipline. Each Hutterite was paid fifty cents a day for his alternative service. For those exempted to do farm work, the colony had to pay the government $15 per exemption per month.

There was another public outcry when the Hutterites refused to invest in government Victory Bonds because the money would help to support the war. The Hutterites then proceeded to make large contributions to the Red Cross and invested half a million dollars in government bonds for non-war purposes. In lieu of paying them interest, which the Hutterites refused to accept, the government pledged to use the money 'to alleviate stress or human suffering due to the war.'[12]

Several times in its lengthy term of office (1935-71) the Social Credit government of Alberta responded to public pressure against the Hutterites. In 1944 the Land Sales Prohibition Act, which prohibited the sale or lease of land to Hutterites (ostensibly to protect them from wartime violence as they moved into new regions), was passed. It was a temporary measure that was to end with the war,[13] but it remained in force until 1947, when it was replaced by the Communal Property Act that prevented any Hutterite colony from expanding its land holdings beyond 1944 limits.[14] No new colonies could be built within forty miles of an existing one, nor could any colony possess more than 6,400 acres.[15] No land could be sold to Hutterites without first being offered for sale for sixty days under the Veterans' Land Act of 1942, which provided provincial assistance to veterans entering farming. There was scarcely a murmur of dissent throughout the province to this discriminatory legislation, though it was criticized by eastern newspapers.[16]

The immediate effect of this legislation was to force Hutterites out of the southern regions of Alberta, where they were concentrated, into other parts of the province. As a consequence, provincial hostility actually increased because rumours spread ahead of their advance and new areas were prejudiced against the Hutterites before they could establish a neighbourly reputation. The long-term result of the Communal Property Act was to encourage Hutterites to branch into the neighbouring province of Saskatchewan and also south of the border into the states of Montana and Washington. Today one-third of all Hutterites live in the U.S. By 1971 there were twenty-two colonies in Montana alone.

Throughout the 1950s there were sporadic but still insidious attacks in the media. The Hutterite practice of holding property in common led, especially during the McCarthy 'Red Scare' in the United States, to rumours that the Hutterites were Marxist Communists. The philosophy of Karl Marx is often summarized as

Communal Property Act

'From each according to his ability, to each according to his need.' This does accurately describe Hutterite communality, but it bears little resemblance to present-day world Communism. 'Those people in Russia and other countries who call themselves Communists are not Communists at all,' said the outspoken Hutterite bishop John Wurz (1879-1960). 'They are Bolshevists. They want the whole world for themselves. They are tyrants who do not believe in Almighty God. They are devils from hell. The Hutterites are the only true Communists in the world and live as spiritual Communists.'[17]

In contrast with Marxist Communism, there is no compulsion to believe in, nor to live, the Hutterian communal way. Marxists believe in economic determinism in human history; Hutterites believe that men are always free to choose their own course. They seek, not to transform the world by 'revolution', but to separate themselves from it and to educate the world by the power of their Christian example.[18]

Manitoba   Various organizations, such as the Canadian Legion,[19] and provincial associations of rural municipalities continued to oppose Hutterite expansion. As a result, some Manitoba MLAs were encouraged to threaten discriminatory legislation.[20] However, the very diverse ethnic composition of the province and better relationships between the colonies and their outside neighbours toned down this hostility. An oral agreement was reached with the Schmiedeleut in 1957 that was similar in detail to the Communal Property Act of Alberta (1947), thus ensuring that colonies would spread out across the province and not, by concentrating in one area, disrupt its business life and educational system.[21] Nevertheless attacks in the media and the legislature led to the government's refusal to allow further colonies to incorporate and made the Schmeideleut's future in Manitoba uncertain. Many more Hutterites moved back to the Dakotas and into Minnesota.[22]

Saskatch-ewan   In the early 1950s the CCF government of Saskatchewan was quick to head off problems that might be created by a rapid influx of Hutterites into their province. When a colony moved into the south-west part of the province, near Maple Creek, and local citizens began calling for restrictive legislation like Alberta's, the government had to take action. However, regulation of land purchases and limitation of colony size was clearly contrary to Saskatchewan's Bill of Rights Act of 1943.[23] The Canadian Mental Health Association was commissioned to make an unbiased non-partisan report on the Hutterites, discussing the probable reaction to the admission of more colonies into Saskatchewan and how mutual hostility might be avoided.

The Hutterites and Saskatchewan: a study of inter-group relations (1953) concluded that 'no society has yet succeeded in assimilating or destroying the Hutterites by direct pressure. The reverse is true. The greater the pressure, the more intensified become the mores under attack. Hutterite ranks close more tightly, group solidarity increases, isolation and withdrawal are more apparent.' Acting on this assumption the Association recommended ways of harmonizing the entry of the sect into the province and into the local communities. The report recommended, and the government eventually carried out, the following projects: a government-sponsored consulting and assessing service to help Hutterites find land where there would be little conflict with neighbours; a community survey to ascertain areas of prejudice; an educational program to counter misinformation about Hutterites; and a Hutterite-Saskatchewan liaison committee that could solve problems as they arose at the local level. An attempt to create a joint Hutterite-Citizens Committee and to promote dialogue between the two groups was largely unsuccessful. The government was willing to sponsor and promote good relations, but there was local apathy. *The Hutterite program: a final report* stated that 'neither group was particularly concerned about the character of its relations with the other. Each group saw itself as a self-contained unit affected by, but not a part of, the life of the other. The primary objective of both groups was the limitation of the other's influence rather than the development of complementary social and economic arrangements.'[24]

When it became clear that Saskatchewan seemed to be having few problems with its Hutterites,[25] the Alberta government was encouraged in 1958 to take a second look at its Communal Property Act. Harsh attitudes were moderating somewhat as war

Alberta: Communal Property Control Board

memories faded and Albertans became conscious of Hutterite examples of good living and sound farming.[26] Moreover, the forty-mile limit of the Act now prevented further colony expansion in the settled areas of the province, and continued application of this provision would mean an exodus of Hutterites in the future—an event that the Alberta government thought detrimental to the province. It appointed the Hutterite Investigation Committee to study the situation and to make recommendations.

To circumvent the Communal Property Act, individual Hutterites had been buying land for communal farming. In 1959, on the recommendation of the Hutterite Investigation Committee, the Alberta government passed a law forbidding this.[27] It also set up a Communal Property Control Board to regulate Hutterite expansion. To protect the public interest, when a colony wished to branch, open hearings were to be conducted in whatever area the Hutterites chose to settle. Then the board would make a recommendation, for or against the choice of settlement, to the Alberta Cabinet. Three criteria were used: a minimum of fifteen miles between each colony, no more than two colonies in each municipality, and not more than five per cent of the assessable land in a municipality to be owned communally.

The subsequent hearings of the Control Board occasionally became forums for rabble-rousing demagogues and hostile mobs when insecure farmers and businessmen resorted to public debate and confrontation to express their opposition to Hutterite expansion.[28] In Warner, Alberta, in 1960, over 300 residents declared that they were prepared 'to break civil laws in Canada if necessary' if the application for a new colony was permitted. One farmer said: 'I'd be sorry to set a match to their buildings and crops, but it's going to have to be done.' General hostility became so aroused that the 1962 leadership convention of the provincial Progressive Conservative Party proposed the resolution that all colonies should be broken up and the Hutterites forced to live on individual farms 'so that they can enjoy the freedom of our country [!].' In that year the government wisely declared that public hearings would no longer be mandatory. The Communal Property Control Board, to the dismay of Albertans, had refused permission to only one-half of the fourteen Hutterite applications to expand, for the sect was wise enough to apply for land where they knew the Board's criteria could be met.

The build-up of hostility in Alberta had taken place over such a long time that several generations of minds were poisoned against Hutterites.[29] The Brant and Vulcan areas of Alberta remain the worst trouble spots, especially after 1964 when a local of the Farmers' Union lodged a complaint against individual Hutterites who were buying land in their district in contravention of provincial prohibition.[30] When police finally laid charges, the Hutterites tested the constitutionality of the Communal Property Act in the courts.[31] Their case was that, 'since common ownership of land is a basic tenet of the Hutterite faith and since only the federal government can rule on religious matters, the Communal Property Act, since it was passed by the provincial government, was *ultra vires* and therefore void.' The case went to the Supreme Court of Canada in 1969, the Hutterites having lost in all lower courts and appeals. The Supreme Court decided in favour of the province of Alberta 'on the grounds that the act governs relations in the ownership of land, which is clearly within provincial jurisdiction.'

Court test

During the 1960s attitudes towards minority groups altered radically throughout Canada, for there had been a vast European immigration after the Second World War. In 1960 a Bill of Rights was established by a Conservative federal government under John Diefenbaker (himself the son of a German immigrant and from Saskatchewan) and it made people aware of the civil liberties of all ethnic groups. Successive Liberal governments after Diefenbaker have promoted multi-culturalism as a national policy and have given more status in public life to people of non-English-speaking origin.[32] Tolerant individuals and organizations have spoken out against bigotry and ethnic groups themselves have become more vocal. Soon unwarranted attacks on minorities became disreputable. Under the shadow of nuclear warfare and in sympathy with those Americans who resisted involvement in Viet Nam, Canadians also became more sympathetic to pacifists. Furthermore, the values of communal living attracted those who feared the anonymity, the depersonalization, and the breakdown of the traditional family that seemed to accompany the massive urbanization of industrialized society. During the decade even the Calgary *Herald* and the Edmonton *Journal*, prominent conservative newspapers, adopted a more favourable editorial policy towards the Hutterites.[33]

Repeal of
Communal
Property
Act

When it first took office in 1972, the Conservative government of Alberta, under Premier Peter Lougheed, appointed a select committee of the legislature to re-examine the Hutterite question. After five months of study and debate, the committee recommended—and the legislature agreed—that the Communal Property Act violated the recent provincial Human Rights Act, which was passed in 1966 and revised in 1971. And so, on March 1, 1973, the Act was repealed. For the first time in thirty years Hutterites were free to purchase land as they wanted. A liaison committee, under the chairmanship of Arnold Platt, was appointed to smooth over any difficulties that might arise between Hutterites and the communities into which they might expand.[34]

The protest march of 300 Vulcan-area residents to the capital city of Edmonton in 1972 was a result, Platt thinks, of his attempts to have the problems of Hutterite land expansion examined by both sides.[35] He stirred up a hornet's nest. The citizens of Vulcan felt that the existence of their town was threatened by the number of nearby colonies and the apparent ease with which Hutterites could buy new land from Vulcan people who were only too anxious to sell out when they could get a good price. Neighbours became suspicious of each other and openly hostile to those who even contemplated a sale. Public tirades against the government and the Hutterites expressed the town's anger and insecurity, but the real problem—*the failure of individualistic farming in a technological age*—was ignored.[36]

Despite protests against the repeal of the Communal Property Act, the 7,200 Hutterites in Alberta quickly took advantage of their new freedom. In the five months after the Act's repeal, 44,475 acres were purchased and seven new colonies established. Colonies have also expanded by 17,518 acres, bringing the total amount of arable land in Alberta under Hutterite control to about one per cent.

Many changes have occurred in Hutterite life during the past fifty years. Only a small number of those Hutterites who suffered through the persecution of the First World War are still alive, and the new generation is accustomed to the style and operation of Canadian government and society. For instance, they have begun to use the law courts to plead civil rights.[37] The Hutterites, and many Prairie farmers, have adapted to rapid technological advances and to new improved methods of agricultural production. Paralleling these developments has been the demographic phenomenon of urbanization—the large-scale movement of people off the farms and out of the towns to the cities. Social change has been so profound, rapid, and noticeable, especially since the early forties, that families and businessmen, churches and community organizations, have exhibited a wartime-like insecurity in finding a scapegoat upon which to foist their frustration and anger over conditions they cannot control. A new version of prejudice and intolerance has appeared. The Hutterites have been accused of undermining the entire socio-economic system of Prairie life.

Their success as agriculturalists is rarely appreciated by other Prairie farmers. The availability of manpower and the access to capital for modernization and land accumulation that result from Hutterite co-operation are in stark contrast to the position of the individual farmer. The lone farmer has been able to manage only a few lines of production, which keep him busy twelve hours a day, seven days a week, for a very low income. It is only with the greatest difficulty that he can muster sufficient capital to purchase new technology or more land needed to farm efficiently. Though non-Hutterite farmers co-operate with each other in marketing their grain,[38] and many buy their groceries and deal with producers and service 'co-ops', and while some farmers work with a father, son, or brother, most usually refuse to work with other farmers—except in rare emergencies. Those who would like to are often not well enough organized or disciplined in their own work habits; nor are they inclined to make the sacrifices demanded by working with others. However, they realize—though this fact is resisted—that farming has become big business, far too demanding and complex for one individual.

Contemporary pressures & attitudes

Amid the jealousies created by their successful farming practices, the Hutterites have also come under merciless attack for buying, at the cheapest prices whenever possible, from distributors. Though it is a common Canadian practice, especially in the cities, local retail businessmen are upset when Hutterites do this and are quick to accuse them of opportunism and of destroying local trade under the guise of religion. To listen to many of the Hutterites' opponents, you would think that they started to farm communally to put small-town storekeepers and independent farmers out of business. John Reimer, a farmer near New Dayton, Alberta, was reported in the Toronto *Telegram* (September 27, 1960) as saying that the Hutterites' faith 'is not a religion—it's a means. Their God is land . . . the dollar is the means . . . the religion simply a cloak to hide behind.' Reimer claimed that in the 1930s the five area colonies spent $14,000 a month in New Dayton among twenty-seven business establishments. 'But in 1937 they changed their religion—I claim it's a religion of convenience . . . a cloak to hide behind—and they started using trucks instead of horses. So they started wheeling right through New Dayton, going to Lethbridge and buying wholesale.' So did many others in the community! In 1960 New Dayton contained one store, a hotel, a Chinese restaurant, and three service stations. Not only on the Prairies, but across North America, small towns have difficulty competing with large urban centres now that the automobile and good paved roads enable rapid movement between farm and city.

While Hutterites may spend less per capita in the local town than do their neighbours, they have a much greater population density—at least ten times that of ordinary farmers. So in total they spend as much as the people whom they replaced on the acreage they farm communally. Moreover, the study that the Canadian Mental Health Association prepared for the Saskatchewan government in the early 1950s gave statistics to prove that, in some colonies at least, spending in the local community was as high per capita as for outsiders. But unfounded anxiety about Hutterites has always been difficult to dispel and their purported spending habits remain a divisive issue.[39]

Opposition to Hutterites is not always entirely economic. Rapid rural depopulation has taken place on the Prairies and small towns are hard-pressed to maintain traditional social life and public services. In 1941 the population of the three Prairie provinces was 2.4 million, of which 62 per cent were rural. In 1966, while the population had grown to 3.4 million, 63 per cent were urban dwellers. From 1941 to 1966 the number of people living on Prairie farms actually decreased from 1,148,240 to 761,067. In depopulating communities the stores go out of business one by one; then the bank and the local newspaper close; and finally the school, the hospital, and the church shut their doors.

When farming was thought to be a way of life and not simply a means of earning a living, there were families who attempted to earn a living on a quarter-section of land.[40] Community projects and a close social life went a long way towards lessening the feeling of deprivation produced by low incomes, long hours of manual labour, and a severe climate. Now, when many sections of land are farmed by one family and the population is steadily decreasing, these amenities fade away, or at best are obtained only by driving twenty miles to the nearest centre. Farm families, feeling lonely and isolated, ask of Hutterites, as they do of all newcomers, 'Are they good for the community?' Prairie farmers and villagers appreciate neighbours who join their social groups and who voluntarily contribute time and money to the annual agricultural fair, Women's Institute, or Dominion Day festivities, and who support the local hockey team and take part in the curling club. Hutterites as yet have not participated and so they are scorned for displacing people who were good neighbours. 'What will become of our schools, hospitals, parks, playgrounds, swimming pools, rinks, churches—all the things which mark our modern civilization—if the Brethren be permitted to continue their expansion?' complained the Alberta Farmers' Union.[41]

The school problem illustrates another aspect of social change in rural Prairie life. During the 1950s and 1960s the governments of Alberta, Saskatchewan, and Manitoba, and of many other provinces, decided that they could not continue to operate the thousands of half-empty one-room schoolhouses that were built during the pioneering era and were still dotting the countryside. Rising capital and operating costs pegged to municipal land taxation, and a severe shortage of teachers, made governments advocate central-ized schooling. Parents in rural areas were convinced by education officials that the quality of education could be immensely im-proved and costs kept in line by building larger, better-equipped schools in urban areas. Despite local grumbling, this major educa-tional and profound social change was almost completed by 1970. However, Prairie-farm parents who lived many miles from a cen-tralized school were very upset when they realized that their chil-dren—even those as young as five years old—had to be picked up by the school bus before eight in the morning (which is before sunrise in the coldest days of mid-winter) and would not be re-turned until it was almost dark, at four in the afternoon. Worse still, the children adjusted all too well to the activities and culture of the school town; their interest in the welfare of the local farm settlement and in farming itself inevitably decreased.

Whenever a new Hutterite colony is formed, the local school loses any children the displaced families might have had, occa-sionally causing the enrolment to drop below the minimum required for provincial grants. When this happens, the school board must close the school and bus the remaining children miles away. Parents are justifiably furious at losing their neighbourhood school and worry about further disintegration of their community. The Hutterites, however, refuse to send their children to town schools; the government supplies them with their own teacher. The farmers angrily respond, 'Why should we send our children [out of the area] when they don't!'

Schooling remains the primary means by which society can assimilate the Hutterites—assuming that a homogeneous nation is still the goal of English-speaking liberal Canadians. However, an Alberta government official has admitted that teachers assigned to Hutterite colonies are often inexperienced, past their prime, or are 'problem' teachers (e.g. alcoholics).[42] Hutterite elders probably are not too concerned about this, as they place little value on public education and are more anxious that teachers maintain rigid dis-cipline. Actually, as the reports of the Saskatchewan Hutterite Committee (1958) and the Alberta Hutterite Investigation Committee (1959) both pointed out, good teachers represent a great threat to the Hutterite way of life. First-rate, experienced, personable teachers might stimulate in Hutterite youth a desire for scientific knowledge, higher education, and an appreciation of the outside world. While public-school teachers have brought a glimpse of the outside world into Hutterite life, thus far their influence seems to have been minimal. They seem to have merely introduced the Christmas concert, Hallowe'en parties, picnics, field trips, and baseball.

New styles of farming are needed on the Prairies. Among the possible settlement patterns of the future are satellite farm villages— not unlike Hutterite communes—that would surround, at a distance, a major distribution centre. By living in close community, farm families might be encouraged to emulate some of the Hutterite colony's prerequisites for financial success: a ready pool of labour, specialization, and diversification. One of the byproducts of this new-style farm village would be the enjoyment of more of the facilities of modern life that an isolated family can never obtain on its own.

There are rural municipalities in which a small number of families (who were able to pool their resources) have taken over almost all the cultivated land by purchase or lease. While economically they are succeeding, they still suffer from the social deprivations that a farm village could eliminate. And in this case a few families are still trying to do all the diversified work that actually requires a dozen people or more. They are over-worked and jeopardize their health to farm, still not as efficiently as possible, the same amount of land that is farmed by a hundred Hutterites. Farmers' unions, which could take a lead in setting up experiments and solving these problems, have found by bitter experience that successful farmers—the ones whose leadership would be needed in any new farming system—are difficult to organize, preferring their individualistic values and their personal material rewards.

Hutterites exhibit many qualities that are obviously well suited to the environment. Other western farmers have much to learn from them.

NOTES

[1] For Prairie reaction to the Hutterites after 1920, see Howard Palmer, 'The Hutterite land expansion controversy in Alberta' in *Western Canadian journal of anthropology* (July 1971), 23ff.

[2] A. M. Willms, 'The brethren known as Hutterians' in *Canadian journal of economics and political science*, vol. 24 (1958), 394.

[3] See the Government of Saskatchewan (unpublished) document, *Treatment of Hutterian Brethren by the provincial and federal governments: a summary* (1963), pp. 4-5.

[4] E. A. Pitt, 'The Hutterian Brethren in Alberta' (1949), an unpublished M.A. thesis for the University of Alberta, p. iv.

[5] *Ibid.*, p. 56.

[6] Production of wheat on the Prairies declined from 3.5 million bushels in 1930 to 1.82 million in 1937. The national farm income plunged from 417 million in 1929 to 109 million in 1933.

[7] The total value of domestic exports was $1.5 billion in 1929 and fell to $490 million in 1932.

[8] Other ethnic groups, however, because they settled in cities, were considered to be competitors for jobs and came under severe attack from local and provincial governments who wanted to prevent further immigration.

[9] Victor Peters, 'The Hutterians: history and communal organization of a rural group' in Donald Swainson (ed.), *Historical essays on the Prairie provinces* (Toronto, 1970), p. 135, states that only one colony was left in the U.S. after the First World War. During the twenties and thirties some colonies either went back to, or branched to, the U.S. See *Treatment of Hutterian Brethren*, p. 11. In 1955 South Dakota again passed legislation restricting the incorporation of Hutterite colonies.

[10] Winnipeg *Free Press*, Dec. 14, 1943; Lethbridge *Herald*, Mar. 17, 1942; Calgary *Herald*, June 29, 1942.

[11] Willms, *op. cit.*, 400.

[12] Paul S. Gross, *The Hutterite way: the inside story of the life, customs, religion and traditions of the Hutterites* (Saskatoon, 1965), p. 121ff. See especially pp. 125-6. Willms claims that twenty-six Hutterite youths left their colonies to enlist in the armed forces (p. 399).

[13] Pitt quotes the Edmonton

Journal, Mar. 17, 1942, and government official Solon Low: 'This bill is just a temporary expedient until an orderly arrangement can be worked out' (p. 115).

[14] Toronto *Globe and Mail*, Sept. 26, 1949. The Manitoba legislature in 1947 stopped allowing the incorporation of any new colonies. See *Treatment of Hutterian Brethren*, p. 10.

[15] In 1951 the province was zoned according to land suitability and permission could be given for Hutterites to buy more than 6,000 acres if the land was not very fertile.

[16] Toronto *Globe and Mail*, July 17 and 23, 1947; Aug. 1, 1950.

[17] Robert Friedmann, *Hutterite studies* (Goshen, Ind., 1961), p. 81ff.; Toronto *Telegram*, Jan. 19, 1960.

[18] Gross, *op. cit.*, p. 171ff.

[19] Toronto *Globe and Mail*, July 10, 1948; Palmer, *op. cit.*, 28-9.

[20] For a typical rural municipality resolution, see the Government of Saskatchewan (unpublished) document, *The Hutterite program: a final report* (1958), p. 2.

[21] Toronto *Star*, Apr. 30, 1957; Jan. 27, 1960; Mar. 15 and 18, 1960. Since each colony has autonomy and no hierarchical or organizational structure exists to coerce a leut or even a colony, such agreements are difficult to arrange. See *The Hutterite program*, p. 9ff. See *Treatment of Hutterian Brethren*, p. 10, for details of the agreement.

[22] Actually this trend started in the late thirties after South Dakota relaxed its anti-Hutterite legislation. By 1940 there were five colonies; eight by 1947; fifteen in 1950; and twenty-seven by 1967. South Dakota retaliated against the influx of Hutterites in 1955 by refusing to incorporate new colonies and eventually passed legislation with a 40-mile clause similar to the one in the Communal Property Act of Alberta. See John D. Unruh, 'What about the Hutterites?' in *Christian century*, vol. 26, pt 2 (July 8, 1959), 801ff. There are now fifty-two colonies in Manitoba.

[23] See *The Hutterite program*, p. 1, and *Treatment of the Hutterian Brethren*, p. 12.

[24] *The Hutterite program*, pp. 1-2, 9ff., and 43ff. There were thirty colonies in Saskatchewan by 1972.

[25] Toronto *Globe and Mail*, Mar. 22, 1958; Toronto *Star*, Mar. 23 and June 21, 1958.

[26] Calgary *Albertan*, Oct. 15, 1959; Lethbridge *Herald*, Mar.

14, 1960. For an opposite opinion, see the Toronto *Globe and Mail*, Nov. 17, 1958, and the Edmonton *Journal*, Oct. 15, 1959.

[27] Toronto *Globe and Mail*, Oct. 14, 1958. See also Palmer, *op. cit.*, 30-1.

[28] Toronto *Star*, Dec. 3, 1958; July 15, 1960.

[29] A public and parliamentary attack has been carried on against the Hutterites by Jack Horner, Conservative Member of Parliament for the Alberta constituency of Crowfoot. See the Toronto *Globe and Mail*, Apr. 2, 1960; Toronto *Telegram*, Mar. 28, 1960; Toronto *Globe and Mail*, Dec. 8 and Sept. 14, 1973; Toronto *Star*, Nov. 9, 1974. See also John A. Hostetler, 'Hutterite separatism and public tolerance' in the *Canadian Forum*, vol. 41 (Apr. 1961), 11ff.

[30] Toronto *Globe and Mail*, Aug. 22, 1953; Oct. 1, 1964; *Financial Post*, Mar. 6, 1965.

[31] Palmer, *op. cit.*, 36, claims that the Hutterites were not dissatisfied with the Board but, because of the police charges, were forced to test the validity of the Act in court. See also the Toronto *Globe and Mail*, Dec. 7, 1966.

[32] Many French-speaking nationalists opposed this policy on the grounds that elevating non-English cultures undermines the importance of the French language and culture in Canada.

[33] Palmer, *op. cit.*, 41. Sonya Rudikoff, in 'O pioneers! Reflections on the Whole Earth People' in *Commentary*, vol. 54 (July 1972), 69, explains that communal movements have become more popular because 'expectations of middle-class fulfilment have been both stimulated and denied, and its values demythicized, denuded, and vitiated beyond recognition.'

[34] Toronto *Globe and Mail*, Nov. 29, 1973.

[35] See also the Lethbridge *Herald*, Oct. 30, 1968, and the *Vulcan Advocate*, Mar. 4 and 18, 1970; Apr. 8, 1970.

[36] For a discussion of this problem, see John Stahl, 'Prairie agriculture: a prognosis' in David P. Gagan (ed.), *Prairie perspectives: papers of the Western Canadian Studies Conference* (Toronto, 1970), pp. 58-78; see also Heather Robertson, *Grassroots* (Toronto, 1973), and her account of the Hutterites, p. 160ff. See also Toronto *Globe and Mail*, Dec. 17 and 19, 1958; Dec. 7, 1966.

[37] See footnote 26 above; Toronto *Globe and Mail*, Dec. 7, 1966; Toronto *Star*, Sept. 14, 1973; *Finan-*

cial Post, Jan. 28, May 20 and 27, 1967. The use of law courts by Hutterites does not conflict with their stated theology of not arguing with another Christian in public, but there is difficulty in reconciling this practice with Matthew 5:40 and 1 Corinthians 6:7.

[38] The Canadian Wheat Board, established by the federal government, is a crown corporation to sell grain at home and abroad.

[39] See *The Hutterite program*, pp. 40-2.

[40] 160 acres. Radically higher prices for farm products in the widely fluctuating year-by-year markets could render obsolete any prognosis for Prairie life.

[41] See also Pitt, *op. cit.*, p. 122.

[42] As reported in the Lethbridge *Herald*, spring 1973 and Sept. 17, 1973. 'About 100 students and parents jammed the Newell County School trustees' office to oppose what they called a "punitive transfer" of Bassano school teacher Noel Sharp to Springside Hutterite Colony. The trustees had called Mr Sharp, of Bassano, in the north-west section of the county, a "trouble maker" in the school . . . and had ordered the transfer on the grounds that Mr Sharp, a French teacher . . . and son of the external affairs minister, did not have a good working relationship with Percy Collins, principal of the school.' See also the Toronto *Globe and Mail*, Nov. 29, 1973. This policy was denied by a spokesman for the Department of Education in each of the three Prairie Provinces in letters to this writer. (Furthermore, they stated their belief that the Hutterites are anxious to receive public education.) The main problem in recruiting teachers is that they do not wish to live on isolated colonies.

The contrasts of two ways of life. The women in the photograph on the right belong to the Dariusleut.

One of the advantages of town life.

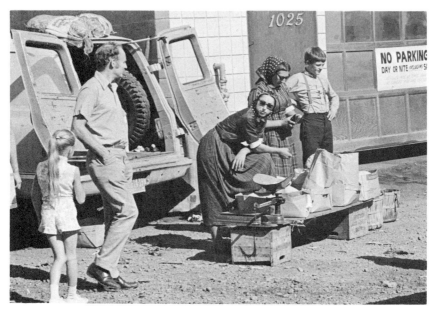

Garden and orchard produce is often sold to outsiders on the colony itself and by Hutterites who drive in the colony station-wagon to a nearby town.

Elderly women stop off for a rest in a city park
on a fall day's shopping trip to a Prairie town. 131

6

A MODERN DILEMMA

For what reason(s) and to what extent should people be forced against their conscience to obey and conform to laws and customs of the state in which they live and are citizens? For what reason(s) and to what extent should an individual or group accept government orders affecting their strongly held beliefs? These are compelling questions for minority groups that try to preserve their collective identity apart from society and for democracies that profess to seek justice for all.

Conformity

Newspapers sometimes carry accounts of court cases in which parents have been fined for refusing to send their children to school on grounds that they can better educate them at home. During the Viet Nam war many Americans who refused military service were jailed. Canada became a haven for others who, for reasons of conscience or fear, fled to a foreign country rather than face incarceration. In these cases the state claimed that irreparable harm would occur and that national security would be threatened if these people continued to act freely. Only occasionally is there a public outcry against such a government stand. When the state decides that its citizens must conform, those who defend their right to act according to conscience must defy the authorities and pay the consequences.

It is in the nature of governments to seek unity and conformity among the governed. Besides using corporal and capital punishment to rid society of dissidents, exile or banishment has been the most commonly accepted and least destructive method of keeping citizens in line. In the small city-states of ancient Greece, an individual—prominent or otherwise—could be temporarily banished or ostracized if, by vote, a majority of the citizens considered him a threat to society. Often people willingly left a state because the pressures to conform were too great. Such were those Protestants who sought refuge in the wilderness of North America in the seventeenth century from the discriminatory laws and persecutions of the theocracies of England and France. Similarly, in revolutionary France in the late eighteenth century, nobles were forced to emigrate to save their lives and possessions in the face of an embittered populace.

Religious and social institutions also have their methods of ostracizing those members who seem to jeopardize the welfare of the entire group. Catholic Christendom excommunicates notorious sinners; Anabaptists resort to 'the ban' or 'shunning' to deal with transgressors. The legal and medical professions temporarily or permanently disbar or expel those whom they convict of unprofessional conduct. Social clubs refuse to renew memberships of those whose presence others find obnoxious.

In short, the right of a wider community to regulate and control non-conforming individuals and groups within it has been widely accepted. It is interesting to observe how one of these groups, the Hutterites, view their relationship with the country they live in, and the limit to which they will allow themselves to be controlled.

Hutterites have a rational and coherent view of God, the world, and their own place in it. They share the commonly held Christian belief in God as the Creator of the universe and of a world that has fallen, through man's sin, into evil—with its values of lust, greed, and avarice, etc. Often the forces of evil that tempt man are referred to and personified as 'the devil'. The Hutterites view history as the continuing struggle between God and the devil for the allegiance of mankind. The world has fallen prey to the wiles of the devil even though, paradoxically perhaps, it is still under God's ultimate control. Involvement in the world, therefore, means to cavort with the devil. One of the deepest motivations for the rise of Anabaptism in the sixteenth century was the conviction that the Church had fallen into sin because it became immersed in the corrupting political and economic affairs of the sinful world. Ana-

Hutterite beliefs

baptism was an attempt to cast aside the influences of the world and to reconstruct a pure Biblical Christianity according to Christ's teachings and as practised by the primitive early Church of the first disciples and apostles. To keep the Brethren clean from sin, Hutterites today separate themselves from the world.

They believe that God, in His providence, has established governments so that the fallen world can rule itself with the least hardship, considering the sin that surrounds and envelops it. In the words of the Hutterite *Large Chronicle* of the seventeenth century, 'the government is ordained by God and is an institution as necessary in this evil world as the daily bread.'[1] Hutterites readily acknowledge the necessity to be good citizens who obey laws and pay taxes. They themselves run their colonies according to strict regulations and prescribed order; their society is a microcosm of the way in which they believe God has intended the whole universe to operate. Hutterites, however, co-operate with governments only when they consider that the integrity of their Christianity-influenced, colony-educated conscience and of their dedication to following the teaching and commands of Jesus Christ is not threatened.

Governments, as well as individuals, at times fall sway to the devil's persuasions, and war—the epitomy of satanic degradation, in Hutterite eyes—often results. Just as there is a line between worldly behaviour and Christian conduct, so, for the Hutterites, there is a point of conscience beyond which the true Christian cannot go in his allegiance to the State. Non-violence and pacifism are essential ingredients in their concept of Christian discipleship and they refuse to acknowledge the right of any government to ask a citizen to kill or maim or to contribute in any way to this kind of action.

Brotherhood

In seeking to maintain solidarity and strength in the face of government dictates, Hutterites call upon a brotherhood of fellow Hutterites—their Gemein—for guidance. Each individual is an intimate member of this brotherhood, which considers itself called by God to serve Him by a form of corporate behaviour that sets the group apart from the world. The concept of individual salvation is foreign to Hutterites, who believe that no one can enter or remain in God's kingdom without his brother. In matters that are not directly spelled out in Church teaching, individual Hutterites normally look to their brotherhood for the proper interpretation of Christian behaviour as opposed to ungodly or worldly conduct.

An edited diary, written in 1918, by an American Hutterite who was conscripted into the U.S. army, illustrates that it is a mistake to think that Hutterites rely *solely* on their conscience, as is common in Protestantism.[2] Jakob Waldner was twenty-six years old, married, the father of four small children, and a member of the Spring Creek colony at Lewistown, Montana, when he was drafted. He reluctantly reported for induction to Camp Funston, Kansas, in December 1917. There he and 150 other conscientious objectors (fourteen of whom were Hutterites) were virtually prisoners of the army for a year. Waldner and the other Hutterites at first refused to submit to the required army medical examinations, much less to shave their beards and put on regular army uniforms. They did so only when their colony ministers, to whom they wrote, assured them that the medicals were not unChristian.

As the government forbade them from having a minister stay with them in the camp to advise them, they consistently refused to do anything at all except keep themselves clean, thus unnecessarily arousing the vengeance of their officers. In the following months they refused army pay, for 'we don't want to stain our hands with this blood money'.[3] They were asked to work in hospitals, on the railways, in the forests, in the quartermaster's stores, the camp kitchens, and even to weed the camp grounds. In all cases the Hutterites always acted together and refused.

An incident near the village of Sobotiste, Slovakia, in 1633, as recorded in the Hutterite *Small Chronicle*, illustrates the extent to which the welfare of the Gemein must be considered by the Hutterites when they are faced with ethical decisions.[4] A nobleman and one of the local Hutterite landlords, Francis Nagy-Michaly, came to the colony and demanded horses, which his servants imprudently began driving off without payment or permission. The Hutterite workmen instinctively grabbed hold of sticks, pitchforks, and axes to prevent the apparent theft of their property; the Brethren's leaders, who might have been a restraining influence,

Hutterite non-conformity

were absent. Some Hutterites were arrested and imprisoned for this affront to nobility and widespread persecution seemed imminent. The Hutterite elders could offer no valid excuse to the authorities. The workmen's violence (or threat of it) was a sin against their own publicly professed belief and conscience. They were reprimanded and had to ask for forgiveness from the brotherhood.

Andreas Ehrenpreis, who tells of this incident, realized that Hutterite determination to bear up under persecution and oppression depended on the conviction that they were doing God's will. 'Even though we should suffer some robbery and harm in our worldly goods,' Ehrenpreis counselled, 'it is more comforting and blessed that we keep our conscience clean and pure.' Any actions that betray Hutterite non-violent convictions could undermine the validity of their communal Christianity and bring mockery and persecution. Thus, if a Hutterite goes beyond a certain point in worldly behaviour, his own society must disown him.

Hutterian conceptions of Christian discipleship have changed over the centuries, for contemporary Hutterites do not feel bound to behave exactly as their ancestors did. The sect, at government request, adopted alternative service during the Second World War and recently, to settle tax differences with the State, they used the law courts. Such swings in Hutterite policy can occur smoothly because, within their highly structured, closely integrated and well-informed colonies, they are able to carry on a daily re-examination of their life and conduct. Similarly Hutterites respond with a common voice and united action to governments when confrontations arise.[5] They seek to live peaceably by themselves, not to bother or annoy anyone. Only when there is no room left for negotiation, when some sort of confrontation with the State is forced upon them, and when peaceful means of resolving their conflicts have failed, do Hutterites take one of what they believe to be the only two Christian alternatives: they flee the persecuting state or passively accept persecution as God's will and judgement upon them.

During the sect's history the attitude of the State towards the Hutterites has also changed considerably. In sixteenth-century

Europe a rigid concept of order and authority was commonly accepted. People thought in absolutes: there could be only one king, one Church, and one social-economic class to which a person would belong from birth to death. The Wars of Religion (1560-1648)—so called because religion played a prominent, although not necessarily a decisive, part in each—and the Thirty Years' War (1618-48) were fought not against the accepted way of thinking but between factions—Roman Catholic against Protestant, prince versus prince, nobles versus nobles, peasants against nobles—each of which wanted to be the sole power and authority in the State to which the other faction would have to accede.

The religious movement called Anabaptism, of which the Hutterites were perhaps the most distinctive part, became a threat to society by challenging not only the prominent institutions of Church and government but also the popular ideas of power and authority.[6] Believing that the nature of sixteenth-century society made it impossible to lead a full Christian life, the Hutterites condemned the Church practice of infant baptism and clergy control of religious and Biblical teaching. They rejected the State's law courts and the use of oaths in legal matters as unnecessary for true Christians; the legal use of force and the government itself were both proclaimed unChristian.

Anabaptists were zealously persecuted. The vast majority of known executions took place before 1560 (804 out of 843), most of them in the Roman Catholic states where the Hutterites originated.[7] Spies were paid to infiltrate the sect, roadblocks were set up to thwart fleeing believers, interrogations and torture were used to force recantations from the Anabaptist faith. Many, perhaps the majority, gave in and forsook their new religion, but hundreds willingly persisted to the death. Some were able to avoid capture by stealth or by fleeing, as the new Hutterites did, to Moravia—then a territory sufficiently outside the power of the Roman Catholic Hapsburg family that some freedom of religion could be tolerated. As the century wore on, the number of executions fell off rapidly—there were only thirty-nine between 1560 and 1618. More and more states tired of the bloodletting, saw its futility as a deterrent, and simply exiled the Anabaptists.

Moravia proved to be a kind of Utopia for almost a hundred years, until the Thirty Years' War brought almost the complete extermination of the Hutterites, wiping out all their 40 to 50 colonies. Only by fleeing further east into Slovakia and Transylvania were some Hutterites able to begin a relatively peaceful new life. But in the eighteenth century, when the Hapsburgs had extended their power further eastward and when the Hutterites had again become numerous and prosperous, they suffered persecution once more—this time in a much more subtle, devilish, and spiritually destructive way.

As a young queen of twenty-three, Empress Maria Theresa (1740-80) was faced with war—later called the War of the Austrian Succession (1740-8)—in which her right as a woman to inherit the Austrian Hapsburg possessions was challenged by Prussia and other imperialistically minded European states. The remaining years of her reign were spent consolidating her domain by trying to eliminate local feudal autonomies and dissident minority groups. A devout Roman Catholic, the Empress in 1759 gave the powerful Jesuit order a free hand to convert those peoples in the far-flung reaches of the old Holy Roman Empire who, with their differing beliefs and customs, might possibly encourage dissension against the centralized rule from Vienna—who might start a rebellion or provide an excuse for foreign invasion. There was no public outcry against this measure, for after the Peace of Westphalia of 1648 European states recognized the right of a Roman Catholic, Calvinist, or Lutheran ruler to dictate the religion of his subjects. While religious toleration was beginning to be idealized by some intellectuals and was slowly implemented in Western Europe, the mass of society still felt that one religion per state was the best guarantee of internal peace and harmony among citizens.

According to the Hutterite *Small Chronicle*, an alliance was made between the Jesuits and the local authorities who curried favour with the Empress to plan a systematic campaign—almost psychological warfare—against the Hutterites. Their methods were to undermine their will to resist conversion to Roman Catholicism and to assimilate Hutterites into the Austrian Hapsburg Empire.[8] First they made lightning raids on the colonies to seize religious books, interrogate individuals, and intimidate every Hutterite. A government decree announced that the Imperial authorities would mercifully pardon all Hutterites for belonging to an illicit religion if they immediately renounced Anabaptism. Later, Hutterite public worship was forbidden and their ministers were prevented from teaching and preaching. By law all Hutterites were forced to attend Jesuit lectures and sermons; at least one Jesuit priest was appointed to reside in every colony. Some Hutterites refused to accept these dictates passively. Abraham Tschetter had the timerity to stand up in church and refute a Jesuit in the middle of his sermon. Shortly after, the authorities spirited him off to a monastery—a fate soon shared by many leading Hutterites.

Finally obstinate colonies and families had hordes of soldiers and officials quartered for weeks on end in their houses. Prime lands were confiscated and sold for a pittance to local citizens who clamoured for this windfall. In one conciliatory gesture, the State allowed several colonies that would accept Roman Catholicism to remain separate as congregations, with their communal way of life and exemption from military service. By these insidious steps the Hutterite Gemein was destroyed and the Brethren were encouraged to accept the inevitability of their conversion. One elder fatalistically predicted, when he heard of the arrest and imprisonment of an outspoken brother, 'We will not be able to maintain our position anyway, and even after long resistance will finally have to become Catholic.'

Soon colonies were bankrupt; families were torn apart. Hutterite membership quickly dissipated. There were no leaders to show the way and no martyrs; there was no direct attack on their nonviolent beliefs or against their communal ways around which the Brethren might be exhorted to rally and to resist. The Jesuits were the only people ever to break down the Hutterite way of life. When hardly more than sixty faithful were left out of at least 5,000, the Jesuits planned to take Hutterite children permanently away from their parents to be brought up in a distant place by Roman Catholic foster-parents. This threat to the Hutterite remnant was the final push. Reluctantly but hastily, the few remaining Hutterites fled

Transylvania in 1767 and went to Turkish-controlled Wallachia (modern Romania), where they settled briefly near Bucharest. Then, three years later, they found a 100-year refuge in the Russian-dominated Ukraine.

The Hutterites' experience with the State in the United States and Canada over the last 100 years has differed from their previous history with governments elsewhere in the world. Not only has there been no official religious persecution, but the State has maintained that religious freedom is a fundamental human right. There have been no executions, no government-sanctioned interrogation or torture, no deportations or land confiscations, no dragooning or abduction of Hutterite children. In matters of religion the North American states have attempted to be neutral.

The United States government in 1917 was under no obligation to exempt Hutterites from military service; it had refused them that privilege when they immigrated in the 1870s. According to law, all eligible Hutterites could have been imprisoned for failing to perform their required military duty but it was requested only that they perform alternative service. From the State's point of view this was an innocuous duty, considering that hundreds of thousands of other Americans, probably most of whom also hated the thought of killing people, were forced to leave their families and fight. By the summer of 1918 the government, again showing compassion and willingness to compromise with religious conviction, completed arrangements to release Hutterites from the army camps to work on farms close to their colonies where labour was needed. The war ended just as the policy began to be implemented.[9]

The punishment and criminal acts perpetrated on Hutterites in American army camps and prisons were often administered by junior army officers without orders from their military superiors and without the knowledge of the government. No doubt there was a tacit policy of not discouraging harassment of conscientious objectors, for the junior officers suffered no reprisals. Waldner reports in his diary, moreover, that several times he received better treatment after threatening to report misconduct to higher officers.[10] And when, on occasion, a letter of complaint was written by Hutterites to the government, the response from Washington

Government attitudes in North America

soon produced an inquiry and temporary relief.[11]

When the government of Canada allowed Hutterites to enter the country in 1918, it guaranteed them military exemption. At a time when there were bitter squabbles over conscription between French- and English-speaking Canadians, this compassion demonstrates the high ideals of the Canadian government. However, the immediate (Prairie) backlash soon forced the withdrawal of the exemption and temporarily cut off further Hutterite immigration —illustrating the difficulty that tolerant democratic governments face in dealing with the prejudices of their own citizens. The government, however well intentioned, was prepared to waver on a moral question during wartime and in the face of hostile public opinion from a region of the country well represented in the governing party. Similarly, the Land Sales Prohibition Act of Alberta —also a wartime act—while it was discriminatory economic legislation, was a temporary and minimal response to the loud outcries for deportation and land confiscation by powerful local political lobbies. In both the U.S. and Canada there has been more evidence of tolerance and enlightenment towards the Brethren than at any other time in their Hutterite history—despite the endemic resentments.

Behind local prejudice and hostility very often lie economic competition and jealousy. In whatever countries the Hutterites have lived, neighbours rarely have taken kindly to their evident ability to make money and find prosperity and have offered little, if any, support for them against government persecution. In the seventeenth century, for example, Andreas Christoph Fischer, the most prominent Hutterite critic in the Hapsburg empire, awakened local anger by pointing out the material successes of Hutterites and their preferred status with the lords.

Economic competition

The Anabaptists have the greatest favour among the nobility. They have the preference as managers of estates, be it dairy or wheat farms, mills, tile yards, gardens or anything else. They are appointed by them to high positions in the castles, such as managers, stewards, and keeper. The lords must pay the Anabaptists larger salaries and wages than the Christians who formerly held the same positions. . . . The lords give the Anabaptists such great freedom that in certain offices they do not even require an account from them. It is displeasing to God that the lords tolerate them and entrust their estates to them.[12]

Their farming, crafts, and managerial skills became well known and, in the late eighteenth century, no doubt made the Hutterites attractive to a Russian government that was looking for immigrants to pioneer regions of the Ukraine. Their success in the following decades, when the region became well populated, again made them targets for local hostility; the citizens wanted the lands for themselves.

Local persecution of the Hutterites in South Dakota in the First World War also took an economic form. Neighbours drove off their livestock and complained to the authorities about unfair Hutterite competition. The state government maliciously took away their charter of incorporation in 1919, thus limiting their ability to do business profitably. Judge A. E. Taylor of the State Circuit Court at Huron, S.D. ruled that the Hutterites must 'disincorporate and sell all property valued at more than $50,000 within 90 days.'[13] Since then all states and provinces (except Saskatchewan) in which there are Hutterite colonies have, under pressure from local politicians and businessmen, passed similar legislation or have had a bill before its legislature threatening that action.[14] The Land Sales Prohibition Act and the Communal Property Act of Alberta epitomize the fundamental problem that has plagued Hutterites throughout their long history. The economic successes of Hutterites seem to bring out religious and social tensions and hostilities that might otherwise go unexpressed.

Tolerance & intolerance

The tolerance and the willingness of North Americans to understand Hutterites seems directly proportional to their distance from the colonies. People who are near enough to Hutterite colonies to hear fabricated or highly coloured tales about them often draw conclusions that lack perspective and are not necessarily factual. While quick to point out Hutterite social failings, they are loath to recognize and appreciate their good qualities. But the Hutterites are partly to blame for this situation because in their predetermined attitudes to the outside world—however justified by past history—they have rarely encouraged any form of dialogue.

It is perhaps ironic that hostility to minority groups has been strong among those who have themselves strenuously promoted social welfare and co-operation as the salve for human problems.[15] Believing that universal peace and harmony can come only by destroying clannishness, old tribalisms, and nationalism, they seek a new homogeneous world society in which all people are equal and none have privileges.[16] To them, groups like the Hutterites, who maintain a separate and distinctive cultural identity, are anathema. The 'tribal' tenets of the Hutterite religion—pacificism and communalism—are particularly galling because they symbolize Hutterite exclusiveness and seem to stand for a belief in their own superiority.

Many people believe that liberty and happiness are man's natural rights (Hutterites maintain that these are divine rights that man can appropriate only by belief in God) and that only by education and enlightenment can man become capable of fulfilling his potential. Therefore the lack of intellectual and cultural stimulus that is found in the Hutterian way of life provokes the charge that they lead a 'vegetable existence' and that Hutterite elders deliberately keep their people in ignorance. Hutterite refusal to participate in government also sets them apart and infuriates those who have crusaded to make people of all nations aware of their political rights, to bring about universal suffrage, and to make it possible for any man to gain a place in government. 'In a country whose basis is democracy,' writes a typical Hutterite critic, 'it is doubtful whether people who refuse to participate in any way in the processes of government can be desirable citizens.'[17] While the Hutterite outlook on life is perhaps narrow and simple, progressive thinkers, in their own 'tribal' desire for conformity, have overlooked the fact that the ability of Hutterites to share and co-operate offers much to the larger community in which they live and that the goodness and virtue they so assiduously practise are necessary attributes in any ideal society. There are many people today—mostly urban dwellers and social critics—who believe this and are attracted to the Hutterites. Being unaffected by Hutterites, and hence unable to use the Brethren as scapegoats for their own economic failure, they see them as a unique group of great value to today's increasingly impersonal society. For one thing, Hutterites have avoided many of the problems that plague the technological age: crime, war, marriage and family breakdown, pollution, drugs, and suicide.

Hutterites are very much aware of claims by scholars and social critics that technology has created many of man's present social ills. They would hasten to disagree with this view, however, for their use of technology has brought about no such results. Accepting it as God's gift to mankind for the betterment of the world, they have gradually adopted almost every useful technological device except radio and television. But while the economic and technical culture of the Hutterites has been slowly modified, their dogma, customs, and social organization have been preserved.

Hutterites claim that there are no problems new to mankind, just old ones, intensified by the pace of life and hence more obvious. Hutterites blame mankind and not technology for the world's evils; human nature is the problem, and evil neither creates nor results from technology. 'The major cause of the startling increase in crime in America is not the invention of the motor car or super-highways or drive-ins,' writes Paul S. Gross, 'but a secular and godless education which robs young people of all sense of personal integrity and individual responsibility.'[18] Youth are given this education, he believes, by adults who themselves 'have wallowed in all manner of self-indulgence'. They want the blessings of technology but are not willing to accept the grave responsibilities of self-discipline that it brings. Gross thinks that the solution to the despair and pessimism of modern society lies in a renewed commitment to God and a communal life of sharing—a life style that recognizes the limitations of human nature and helps people to control them.

The communal life of the Hutterites is the result of hundreds of years of individual Christian commitment and a development of sharing that not only protects the health and happiness of its members but maintains a balance between individual liberty and responsibility to the group. Basic to their way of life is the belief that no permanent good can come in the world—no matter what the political, economic, or social system may be—until all man-

Hutterite view of life

kind commits itself to God. It is idealistic to think that this belief could ever provide the foundation of the urbanized modern welfare state. Nevertheless, Hutterites have successfully incorporated technological change and its material benefits into their way of life without dislocating their society or changing their human values, and in this respect their communes could well be thought of, if not as a model, at least as a prototype for the technologically dependent welfare society that is quickly evolving throughout North America and the world. It is not inconceivable that a religious urban commune, or a community patterned after the Hutterites, will somewhere evolve and give leadership to the larger technological society.[19] We already have the beginning of a pseudo-communal approach to urban living in the vast apartment complexes that exist in our large cities. This kind of closely confined habitation will very likely create new demands on human relationships and responsibilities.

Self-interest, however, is one human quality that works against the development of a harmonious and just social system. Hutterites believe that self-interest is inherent in human nature and they carefully check it in themselves by their colony upbringing, education, and decision-making. There is little such protection against self-interest in the outside world. In a modern state, decisions are made primarily in the interests of the holders of power—the civil-service bureaucracy, the directors of multi-national corporations, and the elected members of a political party—and are modified only by pragmatic considerations of the public tolerance for change. Citizens themselves are subject to selfishness and greed, in the interests of which they often agree to dubious laws and amoral corporate behaviour. Hutterites do not claim that they have eliminated these problems of human nature, or that they have set up a Utopia, but their colonies do exhibit an equilibrium between authoritarian control and individual freedom and responsibility. Every society that wishes both to prosper and to remain peaceful must balance the many divergent pulls of self-interest that threaten to destroy it.

What is the future of the Hutterites in their apparently endless confrontation with the outside world? It seems unlikely that technological culture by itself will bring about their assimilation. We have seen that young Hutterites, like most Prairie young people, are attracted by big-city lights, tall buildings, and the urban pace, and that they go to town at every opportunity, whether enroute to visit another colony, to sell produce to supermarkets, or to purchase equipment. Many Hutterites feel that they would rather live elsewhere than on their austere colonies and that they would like to enjoy the affluence of modern society as they perceive it around them. But their Christian conscience allows them no such choice.

A new kind of liberalism seems to be emerging in Canada. Provincial governments, which have primary jurisdiction over the infringement of civil liberties, are passing more and more human-rights legislation; some, like Alberta, have passed a Human Rights Act. The multi-cultural policy of the federal government under Prime Minister Trudeau is seeking to encompass, within the technological state, islands of ethnic tradition and culture: the Department of Citizenship has set aside millions of dollars of public money to give to minority-group organizations for their own cultural purposes. Does multi-culturalism actually threaten religious groups like the Hutterites? The Hutterites would say that it does. Good times can bring the greatest danger to Hutterites, in the form of subtle and hard-to-resist temptations. Paradoxically, they are wary of those who do not persecute them, for tolerance is but a step towards encroachment by the outside world, and, eventually, assimilation.[20] Hutterites, then, can never escape the dilemma of co-existing with the world from which they have chosen to withdraw.

NOTES

[1] John Horsch, *The Hutterian Brethren, 1528-1931, and the principle of non-resistance as held by the Mennonite Church* (Goshen, Ind., 1971), p. 79ff.

[2] See Theron Schlabach (ed.), 'An account by Jakob Waldner: diary of a conscientious objector in World War I' in *Mennonite quarterly review*, vol. 47 (Jan. 1974), 73-111. Waldner died at 81 years of age in September 1974 after living in the Sturgeon Creek colony at Headingly, Mani-

toba, and having worked for years as a sheepherder and steam-boiler engineer. His wife was the great aunt of the Gross family of Pincher Creek referred to in Chapter 1.

3 *Ibid.*, 85.

4 Robert Friedmann, *Hutterite studies* (Goshen, Ind., 1961), p. 232ff.

5 One criticism made of the Hutterites is that they do not take concerted action to prevent a confrontation but wait until it develops.

6 Claus-Peter Clasen, *Anabaptism: a social history, 1525-1618* (Ithaca, N.Y., 1973), p. 419ff.

7 *Ibid.*

8 This account is based on Horsch, *op. cit.*, p. 79ff.

9 Schlabach, *op. cit.*, 93-4 and 108ff.

10 *Ibid.*, 89 and 92ff.

11 *Ibid.*, 86, 89, and 94ff.

12 Horsch, *op. cit.*, p. 34ff.

13 Schlabach, *op. cit.*, 93.

14 Government of Saskatchewan document (unpublished), *Treatment of Hutterian Brethren by the provincial and federal governments: a summary* (1963).

15 See A. M. Willms, 'The brethren known as Hutterians', *Canadian journal of economics and political science*, vol. 24 (1958).

16 Barbara Ward, *Nationalism and ideology* (New York, 1966). Ward believes this mission to be humanly possible but that its capitalist and communist exponents ignore the slow and profound adjustments in human nature that must be made to bring it about. They ignore man's tribal needs of kinship and belonging etc.

17 Willms, *op. cit.*, p. 391ff.

18 Paul S. Gross, *The Hutterite way: the inside story of the life, customs, religion and traditions of the Hutterites* (Saskatoon, 1965), p. 169; see also p. 161ff.

19 See Benjamin Zablocki, *The joyful community: an account of the Bruderhof, a communal movement in its third generation* (Santa Fe, N.M., 1971), for an account of such an experiment.

20 John W. Bennett, 'The Hutterites: a communal seat' in Jean Leonard Elliott (ed.), *Minority Canadians: vol. 2, Immigrant groups* (Toronto, 1971), suggests that affluence may be the greatest threat to Hutterites.

FOR DISCUSSION, STUDY, RESEARCH

The hats of Hutterite boys and men show influences of individuality and western style.

PINCHER CREEK COLONY

1.   Where is Pincher Creek? Have you ever visited the Canadian Prairies or the American mid-west? Have you ever been to a large farm? Do teenagers live differently on farms than in towns and cities?

How many acres do the Hutterites farm at Pincher Creek? How large is an acre? What are the dimensions of the property on which you live?

In many parts of Canada people are leaving farm life and migrating to cities. What is the rural-to-urban rate in the Canadian Prairies? (See the statistics tables in *The Canadian Oxford School Atlas: Third Edition.*) What is the rural-to-urban rate among the Hutterites? Explain any findings in the light of the information you have learned about the Hutterites.

2.   What are some of the topographical features Hutterites look for when they buy land for a colony? See the photograph on page 1 and the diagram of a colony on page 150. From these illustrations, compare your neighbourhood with a Hutterite colony.

3.   What farm chores do you think young teenagers could do? Do you have chores at home? Is it fair for young people to be given chores? Do you find it nicer to have others help you with your jobs? Why (not)? Are children forced to help with the chores at Pincher Creek colony? Are you forced to do jobs for your parents? Do you think Hutterite children want to help with chores? What would be done if they refused to help? If you were a parent, what would you do if tasks assigned to your children were not carried out properly?

4.   Pretend there are no television, radio, organized sports, or piano lessons in your community. What would you do when you were not in school? What do Hutterite children do when they are not in school?

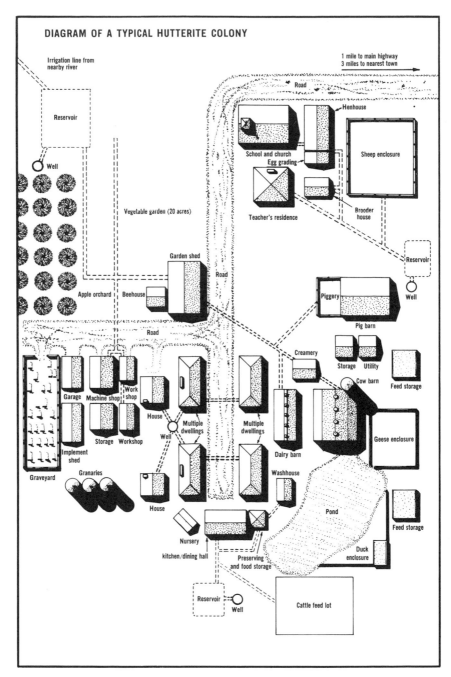

DIAGRAM OF A TYPICAL HUTTERITE COLONY

Irrigation line from
nearby river

1 mile to main highway
3 miles to nearest town

Road

Reservoir

Well

Henhouse

School and church

Egg grading

Sheep enclosure

Vegetable garden (20 acres)

Teacher's residence

Brooder
house

Garden shed

Reservoir

Road

Well

Apple orchard   Beehouse

Piggery

Pig barn

Road

Creamery

Storage   Utility

Cow barn

Feed storage

Garage   Machine shop   Work
shop

House

Storage   Workshop

Multiple
dwellings

Multiple
dwellings

Dairy barn

Geese enclosure

Implement
shed

Well

Graveyard   Granaries

House

Washhouse

Pond

Feed storage

Nursery

kitchen/dining hall

Preserving
and food storage

Duck
enclosure

Reservoir

Well

Cattle feed lot

The layout of a typical Hutterite colony.

5. What time of the day do you think would be most enjoyable at Pincher Creek colony? Why?

How is eating at a Hutterite colony like eating at a summer camp? Why is this better for the mother? Do you eat with your parents all the time? Is it nice to eat without them now and then? What would you do if you were hungry between meals at the colony?

6. What is the role of school-age children in the Hutterite family and community? Does this role differ from your own in your family and community? Explain.

Are Hutterite children ever punished? Why (not)? How are you punished? Are there different standards for Hutterite children and teenagers? What things are considered wrong in your family? Do you ever do things you don't like doing very much for the good of your family? What sort of things?

Are your parents ever punished? Why are adults punished in the Hutterite colony? What sort of things are considered wrong for them to do?

7. Are women important in the running of the colony? Why (not)? Why do you think Hutterites have large families. Why do Hutterite colonies split and form two smaller colonies? How often does this happen? Write a paragraph that explains the process by which a colony 'branches'.

8. Why do Hutterite children usually grow up to be farmers like their parents? What do you hope to do with your life? What influences you in making this decision?

9. Does your grandmother visit you very often? What would change if she lived (did not live) with you? Why are grandmothers important on a Hutterite colony? Write a paragraph comparing the respective roles of elderly people in your community and on a Hutterite colony.

10. What is the traditional colour of a wedding dress in your community? Find examples of cultures in which other colours are worn. Why is a Hutterite bride's wedding dress blue? Do Hutterites choose their husbands or wives? Which colony does a

couple go to live in—the bride's or the groom's? Why? How can you always tell a married Hutterite man from an unmarried one? Can you tell a married Hutterite woman from an unmarried one?

11. Do you speak a language other than English? Do you think it important to learn a language other than English? Why (not)? Are you learning to speak or write another language? Why? Why do Hutterites learn English? What language do Hutterites learn first? Second? Have Hutterites ever lived in Germany?

12. Why is it important that Hutterites get along well with each other? Why do they live communally?

What is religion? What is a Christian? Are Hutterites Christians? How do you know religion is important to Hutterites?

13. How does a Hutterite become a minister? Write a paragraph to explain this process. Why is the minister important to a colony?

14. Why are there no pictures of friends or family on the walls of Hutterite dwellings? Do you think Hutterites like having their picture taken? Why do you take pictures?

15. What is baptism? Why is this ritual important for Hutterites? What decisions will you make in your life that you cannot or should not change your mind about?

16. On what days do Hutterites go to church? Describe their church. Explain its characteristic appearance.

Why is a funeral not mournful for a Hutterite?

17. Who decides the rules on Pincher Creek colony? Write a paragraph to explain the process of colony decision-making. How are decisions made in your family, school, church, etc.?

18. What are the differences and similarities between Mrs Gross's kitchen and your own?

Why do you suppose Saturday is house-cleaning day on a Hutterite colony?

Why do the interiors of most Hutterite dwellings look the same? To what extent do the interiors of most homes in your community differ? Why do they differ at all?

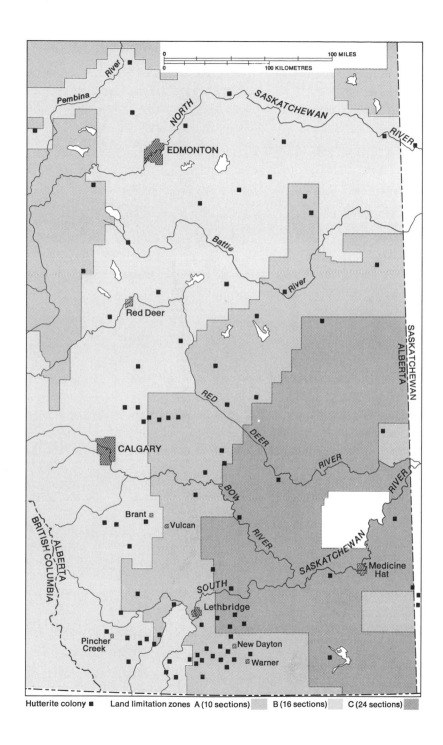

Hutterite colony ■   Land limitation zones A (10 sections) ▒   B (16 sections) ░   C (24 sections) ▓

19. What are the names of the three groups of Hutterites? What group does Pincher Creek colony belong to? Do Hutterites visit other colonies very often? State five occasions when they would make these visits. If you went to visit a Hutterite colony, whom should you try to speak to first?

20. Look at the photographs on pages 2, 45, and 128. Write a paragraph comparing and explaining what you see.

21. If you have long hair, try arranging it in the Hutterite way.

22. Does your mother make any of your clothes? Why do you think Hutterite women make their family's clothes? How do the clothes of Hutterite men differ from those worn outside the colony? (See the photographs on pages 126 and 127.)

23. Explain the nature and significance of dress in other religious sects and ethnic groups: Mennonites, Amish, Doukhobors, Orthodox Jews, Hindus, Sikhs, etc.

24. Estimate the number of adult men on Pincher Creek colony. What do they do all day? How are they organized?

Is money important to the colony? How is most of the colony money spent?

Do you get a monthly allowance? Do you earn it? Contrast the ways in which you spend money and the ways in which you think a Hutterite of the same age would spend money. Why do they differ?

25. How many Hutterites are there in the world today? What happens if a youth runs away from his colony? Is he allowed to come back? If so, under what conditions?

26. Does Pincher Creek colony sound like a happy place? Explain.

27. Write a paragraph that describes and explains the similarities and differences in the pictures of Hutterite children on pages 37 to 47.

28. Study the map of Alberta Hutterite colonies on page 153. What do you think is the significance of Land Limitation Zones?

To understand Land Limitation Zones, you should study a topographical map. (See *The Canadian Oxford School Atlas: Third
Edition*, pages 22 and 24.) Can you observe any pattern of Hutterite settlement? Explain your findings.

29.   Write an essay in which you compare Hutterite society with
a tribal society (e.g. the Hopi Indians). Research the topic under
the following headings: family structures and traditions; the village community; clothing; religious organization; use of discipline
and sanctions; political organization; decision-making etc.

30.   Compare the events of the life-cycle (i.e. birth, baptism, con-
firmation, marriage, and death) as they happen in your family
with those of the Hutterites.

31.   What is the purpose of an 'engagement' to be married in our
society? How long does this period usually last? Why? What conditions are conventionally imposed on the man and woman by
this arrangement? Why are Hutterite engagements of short dura-
tion?

32.   What value conflicts might there be between your family and
the surrounding community—and perhaps your friends? How are
similar conflicts controlled or resolved in a Hutterite colony?

33.   Draw a diagram of your own community. After studying the
diagram of a typical Hutterite colony on page 150, describe what
you think would be the differences between the way of life of its
residents and that of your own community.

   If you were interested in starting a commune (urban or rural),
how would you plan it? How would you organize it?

34.   John Kenneth Galbraith—economist, diplomat, and author
of *The affluent society*—records his impressions of a Chinese
commune (in the Toronto *Star*, July 11, 1973):

Hsu Hang Commune has
20,500 inhabitants and roughly
4,200 acres of land, all irrigated.
This is no great amount of land
—less than an irrigated acre per
family. The crops are grain (two
crops of rice a year plus one of
wheat), cotton, hogs and a variety of factory enterprises.

   The work force of the commune is divided into 121 production teams—the latter being the basic production unit of the enterprise. The commune is, by Chinese standards, highly mechanized with 84 tractors.

Back at headquarters we had tea and a circumstantial review of the finances of the commune. Of the total product, 6 per cent goes for taxes, 25 to 30 per cent for costs of materials, 5 to 7 per cent for capital accumulation and welfare, 1 to 2 per cent for management. The remaining 55 to 63 per cent is distributed to the members.

This distribution must make for some interesting times at Hsu Hang. The first division is between the production teams, in accordance with their contribution to the product. That is relatively straightforward. Each team member then participates in accordance with his recorded hours of work as modified by his accumulated points.

Physical strength

These, on a scale from 0-13 per day, are based on his skill and technique, his physical strength and his work attitude—'whether hard or lazy'. The points are to ensure that he is paid according to both the quantity and quality of his work.

(a) Using one or two words in each case, give every paragraph of this article a heading that describes its content.

(b) Using these headings, make a comparison (perhaps in chart form) of the Chinese commune and a Hutterite colony.

(c) Explain what you think are the goals of Chinese and Hutterite communal living, comparing them whenever possible.

2

THE COMMON LIFE

1. How does a Hutterite colony help a mother when a baby is born? Write an essay that compares child-rearing on a Hutterite colony with that of an Israeli kibbutz or a modern North American commune. (See the Bibliography for sources.)

2. Sonya Rudicoff, in her article 'O pioneer! Reflections on the Whole Earth people' (see Bibliography), claims that the failure of modern communal movement lies in the self-centredness and ego-tripping of its members, especially in their neglect of their children's education and training. 'What really interests the communards is the repetition, revision, and recapitulation of their own experience, so they have no energy left for the structuring of experience for totally new people other than themselves. Thus, the revolution in consciousness may end where it began' (pp. 71-2). Write an essay that analyses the Hutterites' perception of this problem and their solution(s).

3. Rudicoff also maintains that two years seems to be the maximum life of a commune unless it has a solid economic base, extremely strong ideological bonds among the members, and very specific shared rituals agreed upon by all (p. 70). Does a Hutterite colony exemplify these characteristics? Explain.

4. How would you compare the training you are receiving, and expect to receive, for your life's work with that of a Hutterite of the same age?

5. The following is from an article by Lynda Hurst in the Toronto *Star*, July, 1974.

Patricia MacKay, president of the Canadian Council on Children and Youth, recently visited China and came home more convinced than ever that Canadians are short-changing their children.

Mrs. MacKay, 50, a 20-year veteran of volunteer work in the youth area, said that the Chinese system of integrating children into the work ethic at an early age is a more realistic approach to their futures than the Western concept which isolates youngsters from the work world until their education is completed.

'That isolation,' she said, 'often lasts 25 years, until a child finishes university.'

Mrs MacKay, who visited schools in Shanghai, Nanking and Kwangchow with 20 representatives of the Canadian Association for Adult Education, said Chinese children are taught self-reliance and responsibility at an early age.

'They are also taught the value of work—manual work—along with their academic learning.

'At first, I was shocked to see

5- and 6-year-olds spending part of their school day assembling bulbs into flashlights. My God, child labor! Then I realized that what they were doing was no different from youngsters here who assemble blocks in play hours here. Only the work the Chinese children were doing was valuable.'

Once Chinese youngsters reach the age of 10 they have to spend a half day a week in factory production.

'They work quite happily in groups. Honest, physical work is a value in their society. Before any teenager can enter university, he or she must spend two or three years working on a farm or in a factory. His co-workers then decide if attending university will further his contribution to the country.

'China comes first, the individual second.'

(a) What criticisms would you make of Mrs MacKay's opinions of the education of children in China? How do you think the Hutterites would appraise Mrs MacKay's view of the Chinese?

(b) The above newspaper report was followed by an editorial several days later that said in part:

What Mrs. MacKay fails to note is that the Chinese-system is education in the service of ideology, not academic excellence. In kindergarten, before children can read, they learn songs about marching under Mao's banner to crush American imperialism or Soviet revisionism. They get preliminary training for the battles to come with dummy rifles and grenades.

Chinese students are not taught self-reliance and responsibility, as Mrs. MacKay claims, so much as they are taught total conformity to the prevailing doctrines of the state. Questioning and dissent are not appreciated in that school system, and this must have a negative effect on its intellectual quality. The academic diet is meagre in high schools, at least in literature and the arts. They read a lot of Mao and some Marx, and little else.

Compulsory labor for students is intended to keep them close to the working class. This may be good in itself, but there is evidence that the three-year interruption of studies has disastrous academic results for many students. Perhaps one school child in a hundred goes on to university, and academic ability is by no means the chief criterion for placement. A student who has not been a good young Communist, or who has the wrong class background, will not get in.

The things Mrs. MacKay admires in the Chinese way of child-rearing and schooling are part and parcel of a totalitarian system. To contrast them with the fads and follies of a free society serves little purpose.

Do you agree with the above criticism of the Chinese commune? Would Hutterites make the same criticisms as the *Star*? Explain.

(c) The MacKay article went on:

Mrs. MacKay was impressed with the emphasis placed on friendliness among the youngsters. She recalled watching a volleyball game at one school, where the teacher instructed the young audience to clap for both teams.

'Kipling's line that it's not whether you win or lose but how you play the game is truly a cultural theme there.'

And, according to Mrs. MacKay, cultural values are often a matter of semantics. The West's insistence on the rights of the individual and acceptance of competition as a means of gaining success are called conditioning. She wonders what the difference is between so-called brain-washing and conditioning?

What purpose does competition play in your society? What do Hutterites think of competition? How do they deal with it?

Mrs. MacKay also cited the fact that, within 25 years, China has eradicated what was once an overwhelming drug addiction problem.

'I was told they conquered the problem by convincing the people drugs were harmful to the growth of the country and that those who used or pushed drugs would hinder progress.

'The people themselves then began to voluntarily turn in those who continued to use drugs.

'The West has been ingrained with a hate for informers. We've gone so far in allowing individual rights that we allow people to infringe on the rights of others. A teenager here who turned in a drug pusher would probably be more censured than the pusher.'

(d) Are the Hutterites affected by drug problems? Why?

What is their attitude towards 'turning in' offenders of any kind? Why?

What are 'individual rights'? To what extent are your decisions influenced by your friends, your family, your country? What are the most important decisions you will make this year? Will your religious beliefs affect your decisions? Why? How?

(e)

One of Mrs. MacKay's personal concerns is the expansion of children's play facilities in urban areas.

'Cities are built by adults for adults,' she said. 'I honestly think if a visitor from outer space arrived here, he wouldn't know that children lived in cities.

'In apartment blocks, there are legal regulations for parking facilities, but not for play space. There are no play areas for children in laundromats, supermarkets or bus stations. Instead, we expect them to sit still and be quiet.'

Does the Hutterite colony differ in any respect in its facilities for children from the city described by Mrs MacKay? Explain. Do you think that cities should be built for children? Discuss.

6.   Paul S. Gross writes: 'Have you ever heard it said that children raised in a large family are much better-natured than children who had few or no brothers and sisters? It is not a proven fact that in a large family the law of "give and take" is of necessity applied to all.'

Do you agree with Gross's observations? What evidence can you find to support or refute it? There appears to be a trend towards small families in society today. Why? With what potential results?

7.   Gross also writes: 'The lessons of obedience, law, and order should be drilled into the very subconscious of men in every walk of life. The lessons of obedience mould good Christian character, and this is well for the soul.'

Do you agree with Gross? Why? What is the role of family, school, church and other institutions in inculcating 'the lessons of obedience, law, and order' in our society?

8.   Have you ever thought of living in a commune? Do you think Hutterites would welcome you into theirs? If so, under what conditions?

Paul S. Gross writes: 'The great mistake that many people make is in trying a way of life. Christianity, marriage, and community life are all alike in the respect that they should never be tried, or merely experimented with. All three of these "ways of life" are permanent: they demand a complete change.'

What do you think Gross means? (See his pamphlet, *Why community?*)

9. The following is an excerpt from an article by Rosemarie Boyle in the Toronto *Star*, July 10, 1973.

David has warm brown eyes, shoulder-length blond hair and is as active as any 2½-year-old on the block. The only difference between him and the other children is that David lives in a commune and is being raised by five adults, including his parents Richard and Marti Wackerlin.

There are two other pre-schoolers living in the Henry St. commune—and the adults, two single mothers, the Wackerlins and a single man, share the responsibilities of caring for the children.

David shares a small bedroom with Amanda, also 2½, and Alice, 3½. Each of the adults takes a turn at making their breakfast, seeing them off to day-care centres in the area, supervising playtime and putting the children to bed.

It's called co-operative child-rearing and it can make or break communal living when children are involved.

'Major frictions occur when members of the commune have different or conflicting views on child care,' says Dr. Saul Levine, who recently published a report on urban communes.

He is an associate professor of psychiatry and psychology at the University of Toronto and on staff at the Hospital for Sick Children.

Some communes have broken up because parents couldn't agree on discipline or handle the natural possessive tendencies of parenthood, according to Dr. Levine.

How does the upbringing of children in a Hutterite colony compare with the one described by Ms. Boyle? Do they differ? Explain. How do Hutterites deal with the problem of differing parental attitudes to raising children referred to in the last paragraph?

10. A member of the Thomas Merton Centre, a small contemplative religious commune on a farm near Magog, Quebec, explained that most of the group 'are disgusted with the materialism of a technological society. They want to live in a materialistic world and not be captured by materialism.' What is materialism? How do you think Hutterites would react to this statement as a rationale for communal living?

A female member of the Magog community explained: I want to get an environment where people can practise prayer, and the pastoral environment—mountains, lakes—is conducive to contemplation.' What do you think she means? Do you think this person would be 'at home' in a Hutterite colony? Why (not)?

11. Advertising, in attempting to sell a product, is designed to appeal to human nature. The following lines appeared in ads in a popular magazine. How do you think Hutterites would react to them? Why?

'You are sentenced to fifty weeks hard labour every year', 'How to survive school break', 'Compact kitchens', 'Can you guess my age?', 'Country sunshine', 'Good planning and simplicity are back and no one needs a lot of clothes to have a lot of fashion.'

12. The following is a magazine article's lead paragraph. What do you think might encourage this woman's action? Would this situation occur in Hutterite society? Why (not)?

A 55-year-old wife and mother sits down with her husband one night after dinner and says, 'The children are older now and they don't need us anymore. You have your life. If it's okay with you, I'd like to move to a place of my own. I want to start my own life, a life that isn't possible when I am living with you and the children.'

13. The following is from the Toronto *Star*, summer 1973.
Survival of commune depends on rules

Young people who enter communal life believing that they can disregard all traditional standards of behavior and discipline soon are disenchanted because 'without rules and regulations and leadership a commune can't survive.'

Dr. Saul Levine, a 34-year-old psychiatrist at the University of

Toronto, says the picture of the commune as flouting the manners and morals of civilized society is 'fantasy.'

Dr. Levine recently completed a study of 30 communes, 22 of them in Toronto, in conjunction with Dr. Robert Carr and Wendy Horenblas, of the Hospital for Sick Children.

'Whatever the communalists initially intended or practised, in time they discover that to survive, a commune has to live by rules which govern sex, drug use, housekeeping and money,' he says.

'The rules are not too unlike those which govern straight society.' In the matter of sex, for example, men and women fall in love and insist that the privacy of their relationship be respected.

Possessiveness and jealousy are characteristic of human beings in whatever situation they happen to be living.

Drug use in most communes was restricted to marijuana and hashish. 'Heroine, amphetamines and other narcotics were not tolerated,' says Dr. Levine.

Why do people band together in this communal kind of life?

'The commune,' explains Dr. Levine, 'offers an alternate style of living to young couples, small families and single people who feel alone and isolated in the big city.

'The people usually are dissatisfied with conventional living arrangements.

'But they're not content to merely criticize the status quo and the establishment,' he said. 'They want to express their sentiments through their life style.'

A communal living situation presents a great number of potential friction points. Members must work out ways of handling such problems as privacy, space and discipline. Thus, people with fairly similar values seem to get together in the first place.

(a) Why do you think some people want to live without rules and regulations?

(b) Why do you think people in the communes studied by Dr Levine were unable to survive without rules and regulations?

(c) Give other examples of daily-life situations where lack of rules or order can cause difficulty to individuals, groups, or society.

(d) Explain the Hutterite view of rules and regulations and give examples.

(e) How does the organization of the Hutterite commune contribute to harmonious relationships among members?

(f) Comment on the last paragraph in the *Star* article as it might apply to the role of the Hutterite educational system.

(g) Why do Hutterite children not attend the same public schools as their neighbours?

(h) Research the life and society of an Indian reservation in Canada and write an essay comparing it with a typical Hutterite colony. (See Heather Robertson, *Reservations are for Indians*, 1970.)

14.   Obtain copies of German-language folksongs and hymns (in translation)—Mennonite and Hutterite, if possible. Analyse the values expressed through them. Study hymns, taken from your own church hymnal, from the standpoint of specific time periods. How do the words and/or music, to some extent at least, express the theology of the time as well as the religious beliefs themselves?

15.   Compare the mode of worship of Hutterites with that of Mennonites, of other Protestant groups, of Roman Catholicism, and of the Orthodox Church. To what extent are worship and theology related? Can you make any judgements on the relationship between mode of worship and life style?

16.   Analyse the presumed psychological health of people who live communally. Consulting available studies and statistics, compare such things as emotional stress, family disruptions, etc., in the usual family unit with those in communal groups. See the Bibliography.

3

RELIGIOUS AND NATIONALISTIC CONFLICT

1.   In what countries have the Hutterites lived? Where is Czechoslovakia? Why did Hutterites move from place to place? Do you think they should have moved? What were their probable alternatives?

Would you like to move far away—even to a country where the people speak a different language? What problems do you think you would have living in a new neighbourhood and going to a different school? Would it be more or less difficult for Hutterites to move to a new land than for you?

2.   Do you think the Hutterites would put ground glass in the flour they sold? Why might people believe this? In what ways are you or your family different from your neighbours? Do you have neighbours that speak another language? How are foreign-speaking children treated in your community?

3.   Do you think the Hutterites felt lonely during their First World War troubles? Do you think Hutterites feel 'left out' all the time? Define pacifist. What is a non-violent person?

4.   Hutterites read and talk a lot about famous Hutterites who lived many years before them. Who were some of these people? What kind of people were they? Other Canadians also study people in their past. Compare the Hutterites' motives for studying their past with those of other Canadians.

5.   Is there a leader in your school? Are there group leaders among students? Do you find it difficult to persuade your friends to do things the group leaders don't want them to do? Why?

6.   Do you think people are stronger in groups? Can groups sometimes get away with things that one person couldn't? Why? Can groups do good things one person would be reticent about doing?

7. Why do Hutterites live in communes instead of individual households? Why did the Hutterites give up their communal life in the Ukraine? Why did some adopt it when they moved to the United States in the 1870s and others did not?

8. See the passage quoted on pages 141-2 in which Christoph Andreas Fischer criticizes the Hutterites and other Anabaptists when they lived in Moravia.

(a) Fischer uses the term 'Anabaptist' to refer to Hutterites. Why do you think he does not distinguish between Hutterites and other Anabaptists?

(b) Where is Moravia? How did Hutterites earn their living there in the seventeenth century? The term 'lords' implies what kind of socio-economic society in seventeenth-century Moravia? What historical events forced Hutterites to change their way of earning a living?

(c) What religion does Fischer suggest is professed by the lords? From your understanding of chapter 3, why do you think Fischer does not consider the Anabaptists to be Christians? Are there other groups in twentieth-century North America who call themselves Christians but might not be recognized as such by the major Christian denominations?

(d) What are the reasons given by Fischer for the Anabaptists' being hired by the lords? Do you think there are other reasons? If so, list them and explain. Why does Fischer think the lords should not hire Anabaptists?

(e) Write a sentence or two that summarizes Fischer's main complaint about the lords and the Anabaptists.

(f) Turn the following sentences into one sentence and maintain the essential meaning.

(i) The Hutterites were skilled craftsmen.

(ii) The Hutterites had to work harder and more skilfully than non-Hutterites to ensure their position in society.

(iii) Hutterite success in their daily occupations brought them only jealousy and persecution.

9. Find out the differences between Hutterites, Mennonites, and the Amish and write a short essay summarizing your findings.

Another research project might be to explain why, although they have the same religious beliefs, all three sects differ in their daily living.

10. Fischer wondered why Hutterites gloried in their 'supposed' martyrs who, because of their stubbornness and obstinacy, were burned, decapitated, drowned, or executed in some other way. 'Is it not true,' he asked, 'that all Moravia, since it has taken in this vermin, has never been punished so as now—and it can no longer expect any fortune or blessing?' Fischer wanted Hutterites to be exterminated because they were never converted individually to Christianity and yet, unlike the Moslem Turks in Moravia, they made a pretense of living the Christian life.

(a) After consulting the encyclopaedia,

(i) Identify the Turks.

(ii) What connection did the Turks have with Moravia in the seventeenth century?

(iii) What does Fischer mean by Moravia's being 'punished'?

(b) Taking into consideration the presence of the Turks in Moravia and the nature of Hutterite beliefs, what threat might Fischer and others see in the growing number of Hutterites? (They were said to number during this era between 20,000 and 50,000.)

(c) Write a paragraph to summarize clearly and concisely Fischer's attitude towards Hutterites.

11. The *Gazette* of Niagara Falls, New York, commented in 1918 on the emigration of Hutterites from the United States to Canada.

Mennonites [sic] not only refused to fight but their leaders were rapid anti-propagandists, thus helping the Kaiser. They did, however, grow food on their fertile farms, selling it at war prices, for the Mennonite is fond of the dollar in war or peace. The U.S. loses nothing by the emigration of these people. It gains patriotism by their going. We are sorry that our neighbours and ally in this war is to be inflicted with this tribe of dirty shirkers.

(a) Why are Hutterites referred to as Mennonites? Is there a parallel here to Fischer's use of the term 'Anabaptist'? Why do you think the *Gazette* does not call them Anabaptists? What other similarities are there between the charges of the *Gazette* and Fischer? Why did the *Gazette* not express its hostility in exactly the same way?

(b) What war is referred to? Who was the Kaiser?

(c) What do you think is meant by the phrase 'rapid anti-propagandist'? Does the *Gazette* give any evidence to back up this claim? What is the dictionary definition of the word 'prejudice'? Why might the *Gazette* be called a prejudiced newspaper?

(d) What do you think is meant by the phrase 'this tribe of dirty shirkers'?

(e) What do you think would be your reaction to pacifists if your sons and daughters had been conscripted to fight in a war?

12. Describe someone who is 'anti-social'. Do you think Hutterites are anti-social? Why (not)? What is the meaning of the phrase 'cultural assimilation'?

13. Write an essay to support or refute the following statement, using one or more ethnic or minority-group experience(s) as evidence: 'Most societies cannot tolerate any group in their midst that wants to remain separate and distinct.'

4

ETHNIC CONFLICT: 1914−20

1. Conduct a research project that analyses the attitude of Canadians towards ethnic groups in one of the following peak periods of immigration, using newspapers as a source of information: 1902-13; 1923-31; post Second World War; the 1970s.

2. Conduct a research project into the period 1902-13 to determine the influence of Social Darwinism on Canadian attitudes to ethnic and immigrant groups.

3. Examine contemporary immigration policy and trace its development through the twentieth century.

4. We have learned that Hutterites have been opposed by, and in some cases have suffered from, nationalists. In *The maple leaf forever* Ramsey Cook shows that the ingredients of nationalism are cultural homogeneity, unilingualism, a sense of mission and national purpose, a national school system, one religion (usually State recognized), and a 'siege' mentality that attacks forces that divide the nationalistic society from within and challenge it from without. Usually, Cook warns, the obtaining and maintaining of power becomes the sole value of nationalists, and other human values are cast aside or ignored.

(a) Write an essay that outlines and explains the problems Hutterites have had with nationalists in the past.

(b) Should Canadians be nationalistic?

(c) What is the difference between patriotism and nationalism?

(d) Write a two-page comment on the theory of George Grant and others that nationalism is no longer an alternative for modern states because a world technological society has evolved—the world of multi-national corporations and international unions—in which national particularisms are now irrelevant.

(e) If the theory in (d) is correct, what is the future of ethnic groups, of cultural pluralism, of the Hutterites?

5. Examine the historical basis for the distrust and hostility towards a particular ethnic group.

Write a script for class role-playing simulating a historical incident that illustrates the nature of the prejudice.

6. Cultural pluralism is best exemplified in Switzerland, a state that maintains national unity although it has more than one official language and is divided on religious grounds. Protestants and Roman Catholics have been able to live peacefully and harmoniously under the same government, while speaking German, French, Italian, or Romansch. The Swiss do not feel that their religious loyalty or ethnic identification is threatened by their

fellow citizens and are, therefore, free to give total allegiance to the Swiss nation as a common entity that allows tolerance of each culturally distinct sub-group.

(a) Is Switzerland a model that Canada should and could emulate?

(b) Can you find evidence to suggest that Switzerland is not so 'harmonious'?

(c) Research the historical background of Switzerland to find out how the peaceful co-existence of religious and language groups became established.

(d) Are there any lessons here for Canada?

(e) Can you find any other world state that has solved the problem of cultural pluralism?

7. How does the experience of Hutterites in Canada compare with that of other immigrant groups? Research this question under three headings: (a) the initial contact; (b) the first decade; (c) succeeding generations.

Contrast the problems of urban minorities (e.g. Italians) with rural minorities (e.g. Doukhobors) and those who settled both on farms and in cities (e.g. Ukrainians). See Andrew Gregorovich, *Canadian ethnic groups bibliography*, 1972.

8. Compare and explain specific minority-group attitudes towards (a) assimilation; (b) government; (c) religion; (d) schooling.

9. What ethnic groups in Canada have their own fraternal organizations and newspapers? Do they have large followings?

10. Consult the last Canadian census figures (see *The Canadian Oxford School Atlas: Third Edition*) to find out the number of Canadians claiming ethnic origin. Can you imagine why the census-takers do not allow Canada to be given as a place of ethnic origin? Why do you think the government wants to know people's ethnic origin? Why are Hutterites not listed in the census statistics?

ECONOMIC CONFLICT: 1920–74

1. 'One reason that there has been little discriminatory legislation in Canada has been the discriminatory nature of our immigration policy.' (*Report of the Royal Commission on bilingualism and biculturalism: Book IV, The cultural contribution of the other ethnic groups*, 1969.) Research and write an essay that supports or refutes this thesis.

2. Write an essay outlining the form prejudice has taken against the Hutterites.

3. Study the map of Hutterite colonies in Saskatchewan (page 173). What patterns of settlement are obvious?

Study the map of Hutterite colonies in Alberta (page 153). Explain the pattern(s) of settlement.

Trace a map of Manitoba. Mark on it the location of Hutterite colonies from the list below. Compare patterns of settlement in Manitoba with those in Alberta and Saskatchewan.

HUTTERITE COLONIES IN MANITOBA

Deerboine Colony	Brandon
Spring Valley Colony	Brandon
Rosedale Colony	Elie
Waldheim Colony	Elie
Milltown	Elie
Bloomfield Colony	Portage
Fair Holme Colony	Portage
Poplar Point Colony	Portage
Rosedale Colony	Portage
Homewood Colony	Starbuck
Clearwater Colony	Stonewall
Fair Holme Colony	Pilot Mound
Blumengart Colony	Plum Coulee

Interlake Colony	Teulon
Grass Rivers Colony	Waldersee
Bon Homme Colony	Oakville
Elm River Colony	Oakville
Grand Colony	Oakville
Sunnyside Colony	Oakville
Hidden Valley Colony	Austin
Riverbend Colony	Carberry
Hillside Colony	Douglas
Sturgeon Creek Colony	Winnipeg
Crystal Spring Colony	St. Pierre
Farm No. 2	St. Pierre
Riverside Hutterite Colony	Arden
Greenwald Colony	Beausejour
Springfield Colony	Beausejour
Rosevalley Colony	Carman
Pembina Colony	Darlingford
Glenway Colony	Dominion City
Waldheim Colony	Elkhorn
Fellowship of Believers	Gladstone
Riverbend Colony	Glenboro
Oakridge Colony	Holland
Parkview Colony	Kelwood
Miami Colony of Hutterite Brethren	Miami
Wellwood Colony	Minto
Oak Bluff Colony	Morris
Springhill Hutterite Colony	Neepawa
Rocklake Colony	Warren
Barickham Colony	Headingly
Iberville Hutterian Brethren	Headingly
Maxwell Colony	Headingly
Maxwell Community Farm	Headingly

4. Consult a topographical map of the Prairie provinces that classifies land zones according to the nature of the soil, climatic

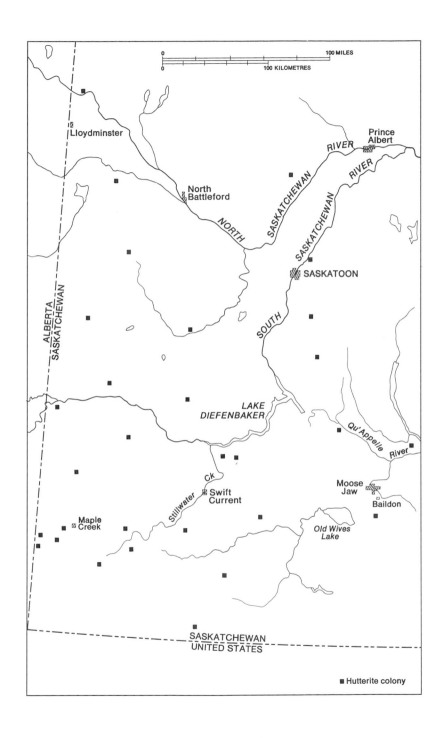

100 MILES

100 KILOMETRES

Lloydminster

Prince
Albert

RIVER

SASKATCHEWAN

RIVER

North
Battleford

NORTH

SASKATCHEWAN

SASKATCHEWAN

SASKATOON

SOUTH

LAKE
DIEFENBAKER

ALBERTA
SASKATCHEWAN

Qu'Appelle

River

Stillwater

Ck

Swift
Current

Moose
Jaw

Baildon

Maple
Creek

Old Wives
Lake

SASKATCHEWAN
UNITED STATES

■ Hutterite colony

conditions, amount of precipitation, and temperature variations. Has the location of Hutterite colonies been determined by these variables?

5. Research the expulsion of the Acadians from Nova Scotia by the British in the eighteenth century and write an essay comparing this event with the Hutterite experience of the last 450 years. As well as historical sources, consult Longfellow's poem *Evangeline*. You could use for comparison other more recent events involving the dislocation of people: the partition of Palestine to form the state of Israel; the separation of the Irish Free State (Eire) and Northern Ireland; the partition of India and Pakistan (or the more recent separation of Bangladesh from Pakistan).

6. The following extract is from a book review by A. M. Willms in the *Canadian historical review* (Vol. 48, 1967, p. 163) of *All things common: the Hutterian way of life* (1966) by Victor Peters:

...the colonies, with their bleak, square barracks are set in bare, dusty yards unrelieved by hedges, flowers, or lawns. The homes have well-washed interiors and bare walls and are austere, without pictures, mirrors, wallpaper, or other ornament. They have no music, no musical instruments, no radio or television; they seldom see a newspaper, and they never have a magazine. The men I knew read little beyond their Bibles and ancient Hutterite sermons, and the few elementary books found in the one-room country school were little use in broadening an education that never went beyond Grade 8. One of my strong impressions is of an ignorant people with little desire for learning. Sports and games of all types are frowned on by the elders. In some ways colony life comes close to a vegetable existence.

(a) What assumptions does this critic of the Hutterites make about a 'good' way of life?

(b) Does this critic ignore some attributes of the Hutterite way of life? If so, what are they?

(c) Some of the criticisms would no longer apply to many colonies. Which conditions do you think have changed and why?

6

A MODERN DILEMMA

1. The supreme court of South Dakota, in a 1958 ruling, upheld that state's 1955 legislation prohibiting further incorporation of Hutterite colonies. John D. Unruh, in his *Christian century* article (see the Bibliography), argued that Dakotans, while seeming not to mind the rich absentee-owners' purchasing large blocks of state lands, acted against Hutterites, who are good citizens and resident landowners. To quote Unruh:

In his presentation before the court the attorney general referred to the unrestricted purchase of land by communals as an 'evil' that the legislature intended to remedy in response to public concern. If the legislature was indeed striking at an 'evil', then, the nature of the Hutterite community being what it is, it was attacking an 'evil' with a religious basis. It is for this reason that many people believe that the question of religious freedom does enter into the case of the Hutterites.

(a) Should the first concern of government be to respond to public opinion or to protect religious freedom?

(b) Do you think religious discrimination is the cause of the Hutterites' troubles in North America? Give your evidence.

(c) Why is there (has there been) animosity between groups of Christians? Between any two religious groups? What answer do you think Hutterites might give to this question?

2. The conflict within Christianity (symbolized by the Hutterite withdrawal into rural communes) over the flesh *v.* the spirit, the church *v.* the world, the secular *v.* the divine, is as old as Christianity itself. Interview a priest or minister and find out his viewpoint. Does he think the Church should be totally separate from the world or deeply involved in it? Why? What are the dangers of each position?

What role do Anabaptists play in the context of world-wide

Christianity? If there is a Mennonite minister in your locality, he might come to your classroom and explain Anabaptism.

3. 'There are no Christian nations. . . . The principles of Christ have not yet been applied to nations. We have only Christian people.' (Nellie McClung). Do you think Anabaptists are right when they claim that a Christian must take no part in political affairs of the world? To find evidence for your answer, what sources would you consult?

4. More and more people and lobbies seek to exert influence on government to 'do something' about various modern problems. Newspaper editorials often demand government action on a wide variety of things. 'Compel motorists to wear safety belts', 'Wage-price freeze desperately needed' are only two examples.

(a) Why do people call on government to solve social and economic problems?

(b) Is total government control of society inevitable? Is it desirable?

(c) Are individual and local group initiatives worth preserving? If so, how can they be preserved?

(d) Discuss whether the structure and functioning of the Hutterite community suggests for the rest of society a way of balancing authoritarian control and individual freedom and responsibility.

5. To quote from page 66, Hutterites have 'drawn criticism and hostility from the citizens of all countries in which they have lived'. Write an essay to support or refute the concept of state sovereignty over private or communal rights.

6. Research and write an essay to show how some Hutterite customs have changed over the centuries and explain why.

7. Write an essay to explain why and how the Hutterites might themselves be prejudiced towards their neighbours.

8. What is the future of minority groups in Canada? Do majority groups have a responsibility to preserve the culture of minority groups?

9. Plan a cross-cultural program in your community or province

to promote multi-cultural appreciation.

10.   John W. Bennett, in 'The Hutterites: a communal seat' (in Jean Leonard Elliott (ed.), *Minority Canadians, vol. 2: Immigrant groups*), suggests some alternatives that may face the Hutterites in the future.

Land is disappearing; sooner or later the Hutterites will have to find ways of either losing people by defection and education, or controlling their reproduction. It is not difficult to see colonies . . . becoming permanent settle-ments which no longer divide when population grows, but who send out some of their young people into the outer world to find their own way, and to carry a modified version of the Hutterite beliefs into secular society.

(a) List the three alternatives that Bennett suggests the Hutterites must contemplate when land for further expansion is no longer available.

(b) For each alternative, write a short paragraph to explain the change that must occur in Hutterite thinking and action before it would be adopted.

11.   Carry out an interview with a number of apartment dwellers to compare their community with that of the Hutterites. Among questions that might be asked are: Is there a way of life peculiar to apartment living? Are apartment dwellers satisfied with their way of life? Why do they live there? What activities, if any, do residents of one apartment share or co-operate in? How long do they plan to stay? What problems exist in apartment communities? Is there any difference in attitude among those who live in condominium apartments?

12.   Consult the materials in a library vertical file and/or periodical index and write an essay that explains the current thought and opinion on apartment living as a model for city life in the future.

13.   What is self-interest? Are you influenced by this in your decision-making? How and to what extent? How do Hutterites regard self-interest? Why? Do you think that self-interest is inherent in human nature or acquired by training and example?

Why is there always a public outcry when elected government officials vote to raise their own salaries? See if you can find a recent newspaper reference to an example of self-interest in an elected official.

What is meant by the phrase 'conflict of interest'? What conflict of interest might there be if (a) teachers sat on school boards; (b) lawyers made the laws; (c) a doctor was the Minister of Health? In the three previous examples, what advantages might be gained by the public that might outweigh the apparent conflict of interest?

Can laws prevent self-interest? Could governments use the same methods to control self-interest as the Hutterites? Why (not)?

14. Select one of the topics listed below for a class debate. Choose a chairman, and a speaker(s) for each side. Give evidence from history or current events to support your point of view.

(a) In time of war, a culturally divided community cannot hope to sustain itself.

(b) A depersonalized society is a tolerant society.

(c) People can look forward to a time in the future when peace and harmony will exist among all men simply because they will be all the same.

(d) If technological culture is to be the 'fate' of mankind, then Hutterites are already practising a way of life that all mankind must ultimately imitate.

(e) Hutterites now provide an example of living and of human values that all Canadians should follow.

(f) Cultural separateness and the age of progress are incompatible.

15. Study the footnotes for chapter five and write a short paragraph explaining the various ways footnotes can be used to amplify and authenticate an essay.

16. Study the bibliography. What kind of bibliography is it? How is it organized? What would be lost by merely listing the sources of information?

Categorize the types of sources referred to in this bibliography.

GLOSSARY

ANARCHIST   A person who believes that all forms of government are oppressive and should be abolished.

ANATHEMA   Someone or something that is cursed, detested, shunned.

ANGLOPHONE   A person who speaks only English.

BENEDICTION   A prayer for God's blessing given by a priest or minister—usually at the end of a service of public worship.

BOLSHEVIST   A Bolshevik—a member of a particular Communist party of the Soviet Union that eventually won power in the Revolution of 1917.

BUREAUCRACY   The day-by-day administration of government, through departments managed by non-elective officials called civil servants, who follow an inflexible routine.

CATECHISM   A set of questions and answers for teaching religious doctrine and practice.

CHRONICLE   A historical record of events arranged in the order in which they were thought to have happened.

CLAN   A group of several families claiming descent from a common ancestor.

CONSCRIPTION   A compulsory enrolment of citizens in the armed forces.

DEMAGOGUE	A person who tries to stir up people by appeals to their emotions and prejudices.
DEMOGRAPHY	The study of populations.
DISCRIMINATE	To act on the basis of prejudice; to show partiality or favour towards some but prejudice or disfavour towards others.
DOUKHOBORS	A pacifist Russian religious sect that immigrated to Canada in the 1890s to escape persecution.
ECONOMIC DETERMINISM	The doctrine that all individual and corporate decisions are not freely made but are entirely determined by the material needs of people.
EGALITARIAN	Relating to the principle that all people should have equal social and political rights.
ETHNIC GROUP	A social group within a cultural and social system that is recognized as having special status on the basis of traits that include religious, linguistic, ancestral or physical characteristics.
EXTEMPORANEOUS	Spoken or done with little or no preparation.
FUNDAMENTALIST	A person who believes in the Bible as a factual historical record.
GENEALOGY	A record of the descent of a person or family from an ancestor or ancestors.
GOTHIC	A type face characterized by broad, straight lines and thick, ornamental serifs. Also called black letter.

HERETIC	A person who holds unorthodox opinions, especially about religion.
HOMOGENEOUS	Composed of similar or identical parts (the opposite is heterogeneous).
IMPERIALIST	A person who supports the policy of extending a nation's authority by territorial acquisition or by controlling the raw materials, economy, and/or government of other nations.
INCORPORATE	To bring together into a whole; to constitute into a legal corporation, as when a group receives a government charter that gives it certain powers, rights, and privileges.
I.O.D.E.	Imperial Order Daughters of the Empire.
MORAVIA	Formerly a province of Austria, now part of Czechoslovakia.
NATION	A large group of people who have common cultural and historical traditions, language, religion etc. It may or may not have political independence and be recognized as a nation-state.
NATIONALIST	A person who has a devotion to the interests of a particular nation or who aspires to national independence in a country under foreign domination.
NATURALIZE	To confer the rights of citizenship upon someone of foreign birth.
NEOPHYTE	A beginner.
NEPOTISM	Favoritism shown to relatives, especially in appointments to desirable positions.

ORDERS-IN-COUNCIL

The method by which a government can issue a legal decree without having Parliament enact legislation on the matter.

OSTRACISM

The rejection or exclusion from society by the common consent of the other members of that society.

PALLISER TRIANGLE

An area of arid land in the Alberta-Saskatchewan-U.S.A. border region, named after Captain John Palliser, who first surveyed the Canadian Prairies in 1857.

PEDAGOGUE

A teacher, especially one who instructs in a dogmatic or pedantic manner.

PRAGMATIC

Treating facts, thoughts, and actions with reference to their practical results or lessons.

PREJUDICE

A preconceived preference or idea.

SECT

A group that holds common religious beliefs, usually different from those of an established Church from which it has separated.

SECULAR

Belonging to the world, worldly; commonly used to mean not spiritual or religious.

SLOVAKIA

The eastern region, and a former province, of Czechoslovakia.

SOCIAL CREDIT

An intricate monetary scheme that includes the theory that industrial profits should be returned to the community as a whole in the form of dividends paid to consumers by the government.

TRAUMA

An emotional shock that creates lasting damage to one's psychological development.

TRIBE — A social organization or centralized political unit made up of bands or other small groups sharing a common language, culture, and ancestry.

TYROL — An alpine region of western Austria and northern Italy; a province of Austria.

ULTRA VIRES — Beyond authority (e.g. of the government).

UTOPIA — An imaginary island, described by Sir Thomas More in a book of that name (1516), with a perfect social and political system.

WOMEN'S INSTITUTE — A rural women's organization for friendship and social service that is open to all.

BIBLIOGRAPHY

A more complete bibliography of books, articles, and theses on the Hutterites can be found in John W. Bennett, *Hutterian Brethren: the agricultural economy and social organization of a communal people* (Stanford, Calif., 1967), pp. 281-8. For a thorough bibliography on communal living see Benjamin Zablocki, *The joyful community* (Baltimore, Md, 1971), pp. 335-42.

Bach, Marcus. *Strange sects and curious cults*. New York, 1962. See chapter 17, 'The Hutterites', in which the author suggests that, although the Hutterites are the only 'utopian experimenters' to succeed in North America, there are signs that they are being culturally assimilated.

Bennett, John W. *Hutterian Brethren: the agricultural economy and social organization of a communal people*. Stanford, Calif., 1967. The author concludes, in this clearly written sociological and anthropological study of southwestern Saskatchewan Hutterites, that they have been able to maintain their historic communal integrity by 'good management', a 'strong social system', and a 'clear sense of cultural identity'.

————. 'The Hutterites: a communal seat' in Jean Leonard Elliott, ed., *Minority Canadians: vol. 2, Immigrant groups*. Toronto, 1971. Here Bennett maintains that the intolerance accorded Hutterites often stems from their 'aloof', 'different', and 'foreign-like' appearance. This may be overcome as Hutterite population growth causes them to send out missionaries (even to urban areas) and thus, contacts grow with the external world.

Clasen, Claus-Peter, *Anabaptism: a social history, 1525-1618*. Ithaca, N.Y., 1973. Chapter 8, 'The Hutterites', sets the communal beginnings of the group within the larger context of the sixteenth-century religious phenomenon of Anabaptism, using government and church records as primary source material.

Dickens, A. G. *Reformation and society in sixteenth century Europe*. London, 1966. This is an unsympathetic treatment of the nature of Anabaptism and its place within Reformation society using traditional secondary source material.

Eaton, Joseph W. and Albert J. Mayer. *Man's capacity to reproduce: the demography of a unique population*. New York, 1954. Reprinted from *Human Biology*, vol. 25, no. 3. A close study of the Hutterites and their high birth rate.

—— and Robert J. Weil. *Culture and mental disorders: a comparative study of Hutterites and other populations*. New York, 1955. A pioneering study based on careful observation of Hutterites and statistical studies showing the emotional well-being of Hutterite communal life.

Friedmann, Robert. *Hutterite studies*. Goshen, Ind., 1961. The author's thorough examination of ancient Hutterite manuscripts and chronicles has enabled him to write a lucid explanation of the sect's Christian theology and practice.

Gross, Paul S. *Hutterian Brethren, life and religion*. Pincher Creek, undated. A sermon-like, Biblically oriented pamphlet explanation of the Hutterite faith.

——. *The Hutterite way: the inside story of the life, customs, religion and traditions of the Hutterites*. Saskatoon, 1965.

——. *Why community? The Christian community: the idea of communal living*. Espanola, Wash., undated. Gross relates Hutterite family life and the problems of raising children to the ideals of communal living as Hutterites perceive them in the teachings of Christ. A list of other writings by Gross may be obtained from the author: Paul S. Gross, Rt 1, P.O. Box 6E, Rearden, Wash. 99029, U.S.A.

Horsch, John. *The Hutterian Brethren, 1528-1931, and the principle of non-resistance as held by the Mennonite Church*. Goshen,

Ind., 1931; reprinted 1971. A study of Hutterite faith and history (emphasizing the period before 1770) using the various Hutterite chronicles and non-Hutterite primary sources of the Austrian Hapsburg empire.

Hostetler, John A. and Gertrude Enders Huntington. *The Hutterites in North America.* Stanford, Calif., 1967. This book is a cultural anthropological examination that views 'the principle of order as a key concept underlying the Hutterite way of life'. This order permeates their society and is inculcated through their language, religion, housing, and educational system.

Palmer, Howard. *Land of the second chance.* Lethbridge, Alta, 1972. A chapter on the Hutterites is included in this comprehensive historical and sociological study of ethnic groups in southern Alberta. Palmer examines the influence of the province on these groups and their impact on Alberta.

Peters, Victor. *All things common: the Hutterian way of life.* Minneapolis, Minn., 1966. A readable sociological analysis set in a historical context that is now available in paperback.

———. 'The Hutterians: history and communal organization of a rural group' in Donald Swainson, ed., *Historical essays on the Prairie provinces.* Toronto, 1970. Peters suggests that Hutterite values are largely acceptable to Canadians and that the sect could, in time, be considered a valuable component of the Canadian mosaic.

Robertson, Heather. *Grass-roots.* Toronto, 1973. Pages 160 to 164 contain a flippant yet keenly analytical glimpse into the Hutterite colony at Miami, Man., and into the attitudes of Manitobans towards this group.

Tschetter, Peter S. *Hutterian Brethren of yesterday and today.* Minburn, Alta, 1966. A pamphlet containing two Hutterite sermons, one of them on the Lord's Prayer.

Zablocki, Benjamin. *The joyful community: an account of the Bruderhof, a communal movement now in its third generation.* Baltimore, Md, 1971. This paperback is an important study of a large religious communal organization that was once part of the Church of the Hutterian Brethren but was expelled when it undertook work in urban areas. Before a young adult, who has grown up within the Bruderhof, can be baptized and accepted into the community he must spend two years in the outside world.

PERIODICAL ARTICLES AND UNPUBLISHED HUTTERITE STUDIES

Allard, William Albert. 'The Hutterites, plain people of the west' in *National geographic*, vol. 138, no. 1, 124ff.

Brattrud, Audrey and S. C. Lee. 'Marriage under a monastic mode: a preliminary report on the Hutterite family in South Dakota' in *Journal of marriage and the family*, vol. 29, Aug. 1967, 512ff.

Canadian Mental Health Association. *The Hutterites and Saskatchewan: a study of inter-group relations.* Unpublished. Regina, 1953.

Cook, Robert C. 'The North American Hutterites: a study in human multiplication' in *Population bulletin*, vol. 10, Dec. 1954, 97-107.

Eaton, Joseph W. 'Controlled acculturation: a survival technique of the Hutterites' in *American sociological review*, no. 17, 1952, 331-40.

——— and Robert J. Weil. 'The mental health of the Hutterites' in *Scientific American*, vol. 189, no. 6, Dec. 1953.

Epp, Frank H. 'Canada and the American draft-dodger in World War I', a paper prepared for the 51st annual meeting of the Canadian Historical Association, Montreal, 1972.

Friedmann, Robert. 'Hutterite education' in the *Mennonite encyclopaedia*. This four-volume encyclopedia has other pertinent articles on the Hutterites.

Government of Alberta. *Report of the Hutterite Investigation Committee.* Unpublished. Edmonton, 1959.

Government of Saskatchewan. *The Hutterite program: a final report*. Unpublished document. Saskatoon, 1958.

———. *Treatment of Hutterian Brethren by provincial and federal governments: a summary*. Unpublished document, 1963.

Hostetler, John A. 'Hutterite separatism and public tolerance' in *Canadian Forum*, vol. 41, Apr. 1961, 11ff.

———. 'Socialization and adaptations to public schooling: the Hutterian Brethren and the Old Order Amish' in the *Sociological quarterly*, vol. 11, spring 1970, 194ff.

Knill, William D. 'The Hutterites: cultural transmission in a closed society', a paper presented to the Centennial Conference on the history of the Canadian West, Banff, Alta, 1967.

Mann, George. 'Functional autonomy among English school teachers in the Hutterite colonies of southern Alberta: a study of social control'. University of Colorado, unpublished Ph.D. thesis, 1974.

Mitchell, W. O. 'The people who don't want equality' in *Maclean's*, July 3, 1965.

Palmer, Howard. 'The Hutterite land expansion controversy in Alberta' in *Western Canadian journal of anthropology*, July 1971, 18-46.

Pitt, Edwin A. 'The Hutterite Brethren in Alberta'. University of Alberta, unpublished M.A. thesis, 1949.

Russell, George. 'The Hutterite colony: a world apart. Bound together in the fear of a harsh God' in *Weekend*, vol. 24, no. 14, Apr. 6, 1974.

Sawka, Patricia. 'The Hutterite way of life' in the *Canadian geographic journal*, Oct. 1968, 127ff.

Schlabach, Theron, ed. 'An account by Jakob Waldner: diary of a conscientious objector in World War I' in *Mennonite quarterly review*, vol. 47, Jan. 1974, 73-111.

Steele, C. Frank. 'Canada's Hutterite settlement' in the *Canadian geographic journal,* vol. 22, June 1941, 309-14.

Swan, Jon. 'The 400-year-old commune' in the *Atlantic monthly,* vol. 230, Nov. 1972, 90-100.

Thomas, Norman. 'The Hutterian Brethren' in *South Dakota historical collections,* vol. 25, 1951, 265-99.

Unruh, John D. 'What about the Hutterites?' in the *Christian century,* vol. 26, pt 2, July 8, 1959, 801ff.

Willms, A. M. 'The Brethren known as Hutterians' in *Canadian journal of economics and political science,* vol. 24, 1958, 391ff.

Wilson, Bryan R. 'The migrating sects' in the *British journal of sociology,* vol. 18, Sept. 1967, 303-17.

INDEX